Music Talks with Children

by Thomas Tapper

Originally published in 1897.

TO THE CHILDREN AT HOME

"Teach me to live! No idler let me be,

But in Thy service hand and heart employ."

—BAYARD TAYLOR

PREFACE

A book of this kind, though addressed to children, must necessarily reach them through an older person. The purpose is to suggest a few of the many aspects which music may have even to the mind of a child. If these chapters, or whatever may be logically suggested by them, be actually used as the basis of simple Talks with children, music may become to them more than drill and study. They should know it as an art, full of beauty and of dignity; full of pure thought and abounding in joy. Music with these characteristics is the true music of the heart. Unless music gives true pleasure to the young it may be doubted if it is wisely studied.

Our failure to present music to the young in a manner that interests and holds them is due not so much to the fact that music is too difficult for children, but because the children themselves are too difficult for us. In our ignorance we often withhold the rightful inheritance. We must not forget that the slower adult mind often meets a class of difficulties which are not recognized by the unprejudiced child. It is not infrequent that with the old fears in us we persist in recreating difficulties.

There should be ever present with the teacher the thought that music must be led out of the individuality, not driven into it.

The teacher's knowledge is not a hammer, it is a light.

While it is suggested that these chapters be used as the subject-matter for talks with the children, they may read verbatim if desired. All foot-note references and suggestions are addressed to the older person—the mother or the teacher. There is much in the literature of art that would interest children if given to them discriminatingly.

THOMAS TAPPER

BOSTON, October 30, 1896

CONTENTS

PREFACE

I. WHAT THE FACE TELLS

II. WHY WE SHOULD STUDY MUSIC

III. MUSIC IN THE HEART

IV. THE TONES ABOUT US

V. LISTENING

VI. THINKING IN TONE

VII. WHAT WE SEE AND HEAR

VIII. THE CLASSICS

IX. WHAT WE SHOULD PLAY

X. THE LESSON

XI. THE LIGHT ON THE PATH

XII. THE GREATER MASTERS

XIII. THE LESSER MASTERS

XIV. HARMONY AND COUNTERPOINT

XV. MUSIC AND READING

XVI. THE HANDS

XVII. WHAT THE ROMAN LADY SAID

XVIII. THE GLORY OF THE DAY

XIX. THE IDEAL

XX. THE ONE TALENT

XXI. LOVE FOR THE BEAUTIFUL

XXII. IN SCHOOL

XXIII. MUSIC IN SCHOOL

XXIV. HOW ONE THING HELPS ANOTHER

XXV. THE CHILD AT PLAY

APPENDIX

BY THE SAME AUTHOR.

Chats with Music Students; or Talks about Music and Music Life.

"A remarkably valuable work. It is made up of talks to students, calculated to make them think; of hints and suggestions which will be of immense assistance to those who are earnestly trying to become proficient in music."—Boston Transcript.

"No other book covers the same broad field which this covers in such a pleasant and inspiring manner."—The Writer (Boston).

The Music Life and How to Succeed in it.

"These ideas are worthy of attention from students and workers in all branches of art, science, and literature, who mean to be serious and earnest."—Boston Transcript.

"Exceedingly valuable because of its broad impartiality in its exposition of truth, its depth of understanding, and, above all, for its earnest desire, manifest in every word, to lead music students to a love for music itself.... It abounds in high artistic thought and insight."—The Boston Times.

CHAPTER I.

WHAT THE FACE TELLS.

"And the light dwelleth with him."—Daniel II: 22.

Once a master said to a child:

"If thou wilt study diligently, learn, and do good unto others, thy face shall be filled with light."

So the child studied busily, learned, and sought how she could do good unto others. And every little while she ran to the glass to see if the light was coming. But at each time she was disappointed. No light was there. Try as faithfully as she would, and look as often as she would, it was always the same.

I do not know if she doubted the master or not; but it is certain she did not know what to make of it. She grieved, and day after day her disappointment grew. At length she could bear it no longer, so she went to the master and said:

"Dear master, I have been so diligent! I have tried to learn and to do good unto others. Yet every time I have sought in my face the light which you promised, it has not been there. No, not a single time."

Now the master listened intently, and watching her face as she spoke, he said:

"Thou poor little one, in this moment, as thou hast spoken to me, thy face has been so filled with light that thou wouldst not believe. And dost thou know why? It is because every word thou hast spoken in this moment has come from thy heart.

"Thou must learn in the first days this lesson: When the thought and the deed are in the heart, then the light is in the face, always, and it is there at no other time. It could not be. And what is in thy heart when thou art before the glass? In that moment hast thou turned away from diligence, and from learning, and from the love of doing good unto others and in thy heart there is left only the poor curiosity to see the light which can never shine when it is sought. Thou canst never see the light of thy own face. For thee that light is forever within, and it will not prosper thy way to want to look upon it. It is only as thou art faithful that this is added unto thee."

Sorrowing yet more than before the little child said:

"Master, I do not understand what thou hast said, yet I believe thee; but the wish is yet within me to see the light of my face, if only for once. Thou who art wise, tell me why it is denied me."

And the master made answer:

"It is denied to us all. No one may see the light of his own face. Therefore thou shalt labor daily with diligence that thy light shall shine before others. And if thou wouldst see the light thou shalt cause it to shine in another. That is the greatest of all—to bring forth the light. And to do this, thou shalt of thyself be faithful in all things. By what thou art thou must show diligence, the love for learning, and the desire to do good unto others, even as these things have been taught thee."

CHAPTER II.

WHY WE SHOULD STUDY MUSIC

"Music makes people more gentle and meek, more modest and understanding."—Martin Luther [1]

It was this same music lover who said once, "Music is the fairest gift of God." Just these words should be a sufficient answer to the question which we have asked in this Talk, but a little more may make it clearer. Here we are, gathered together to talk about music. We know music is pleasing; to many of us it is even more than a pleasure; of course, it is difficult to get the lessons properly and we must struggle and strive. Often the way seems so rude and stony that we cannot advance. We are hurt, and hot tears of discouragement come, and we sit down dejected feeling it were best never to try again. But even when the tears flow the fastest we feel something within us which makes us listen. We can really hear our thoughts battling to tell us something,—prompted by the heart, we may be sure.

And what is music making our thoughts say?

"Have I not been a pleasure and a comfort to you? Have I not set you to singing and to dancing many and many times? Have I not let you sing your greatest happiness? And am I not ever about you, at home, in school, in church? even in the streets I have never deserted you. Always, always I have made you merry. But this was music you heard. Now you have said you wished to know me yourself; to have me come to dwell in your heart that you might have me understandingly, and because I ask labor of you for this, you sit here with your hot tears in your eyes and not a bit of me present in your heart. Listen! Am I not there? Yes, just a bit. Now more and more, and now will you give me up because I make you work a little?"

Well, we all have just this experience and we always feel ashamed of our discouragements; but even this does not tell us why we should study music. Some people study it because they have to do so; others because they love it. Surely it must be best with those who out of their hearts choose to learn about tones and the messages they tell.

Did you ever notice how people seem willing to stop any employment if music comes near? Even in the busiest streets of a city the organ-man will make us listen to his tunes. In spite of the hurry and the crowd and the jumble of noises, still the organ-tones go everywhere clear, full, melodious, bidding us heed them. Perhaps we mark the music with the hand, or walk differently, or begin to sing with it. In one way or another the music will make us do something—that shows its power. I have seen in many European towns a group of children about the organ-man,[2] dancing or singing as he played and enjoying every tune to the utmost. This taught me that music of every kind has its lover, and that with a little pains and a little patience the love for music belongs to all alike, and may be increased if other things do not push it aside.

Now, one of the first things to be said of music is that it makes happiness, and what makes happiness is good for us, because happiness not only lightens the heart, but it is one of the best ways to make the light come to the face. The moment we study music we learn a severe lesson, and that is this: There can be no use in our trying to be musicians unless we are willing to learn perfect order in all the music-tasks we do.

In this, music is a particularly severe mistress. Nothing slovenly, untidy, or out of order will do. The count must be absolutely right, not fast nor slow as our fancy dictates, but even and regular. The hands must do their task together in a friendly manner; the one never crowding nor hurrying the other, each willing to yield to the other when the right moment comes.[3] The feet must never use the pedals so as to make the harmonies mingle wrongly, but at just the right moment must make the strings sing together as the composer desires. The thoughts can never for a single moment wander from the playing; they must remain faithful, preparing what is to come and commanding the hands to do exactly the right task in the right way. That shows us, you see, the second quality and a strict one of music. It will not allow us to be disorderly, and more than this, it teaches us a habit for order that will be a gain to us in every other task. Now let us see:

First, we should study music for the happiness it will give us.

Second, we should study music for the order it teaches us.

There is a third reason. If music gives us happiness, do we not in learning it gain a power to contribute happiness to others? That is one of the greatest pleasures in learning. Not only does the knowledge prove of use and joy to us, but we can constantly make it useful and joy-giving to others. Does this not teach us how thankful we should be to all those who live usefully? And think of all the men who have passed their lives writing beautiful thoughts, singing out of their very hearts, day after day, all their life long, for the joy of others forever after.

In our next Talk we shall learn that pure thought, written out of the heart, is forever a good in the world. From this we shall learn that to study music rightly is to cultivate in our own hearts the same good thought which the composer had. Hence the third reason we can find for studying music is that it makes us able to help and to cheer others, to help them by willingly imparting the little knowledge we have, and to cheer them by playing the beautiful thoughts in tone which we have learned.

These are three great reasons, truly, but there are many others. Let us speak about one of them. In some of the Talks we are to have we shall learn that true music comes from a true heart; and that great music—that is the classics—is the thought of men who are pure and noble, learned in the way to write, and anxious never to write anything but the best. There is plainly a great deal of good to us if we study daily the music of men such as these. In this way we are brought in touch with the greatest thought. This constant presence and influence will mold our thoughts to greater strength and greater beauty. When we read the history of music, we shall see that the greatest composers have always been willing to study in their first days the master works of their time. They have strengthened their thoughts by contact with thoughts stronger than their own, and we may gain in just the same way if we will. We know now that there are many reasons why it is good for us to study music. We have spoken particularly of four of these. They are:

First, for the happiness it will give us.

Second, for the order it demands of us.

Third, for the power it gives us to help and cheer others.

Fourth, for the great and pure thought it brings before us and raises in us.

All these things, are they true, you ask? If the little child had asked that of the master he would have said:

"These things shalt thou find real because they make thee brave. And the pain and the drudgery and the hot tears shall be the easier to bear for this knowledge, which should be strong within thee as a pure faith."

CHAPTER III.

MUSIC IN THE HEART

"Raffaello's genius goes directly to the heart."—
Autobiography of Benvenuto Cellini [4]

The only true way to learn is by doing. The skill of the hand and the skill of the thought can be brought out only by use. We shall not become very skilful, nor very learned, nor very good unless we daily devote ourselves to tasks—often difficult and unpleasant—which shall bring to us wisdom, or success, or goodness. None of these things, nor any other like them, come merely by talking about them. That is the worst way of all—merely to talk and not to act. But if we talk truthfully and act with care, we shall gain a great deal. Pleasant companionship often brings forth thoughts which if we follow them industriously, lead a long way in a good direction.

I do not know that any one has likened music to a country. But we can make the comparison, and then it becomes plain that we may either wander through it, seeing the beautiful things, wondering about them, and talking over our admiration and our wonder; or we may join to this a true and an earnest inquiry, which shall give us, as a reward, the clear understanding of some things which we see. Let us travel in this way; first, because we shall gain true knowledge by it, but better still, because we shall thereby learn in the first days that the truest pleasures and the dearest happinesses are those for which we have done something; those for which we have given both of labor and of pains.

One of the wisest little philosophers in the world was Polissena,[5] and I think she became wise just because she labored. As we become more and more acquainted with true music we shall learn this: True music is that which is born in some one's heart. "All immortal writers speak out of the heart."[6] Nothing could be truer; and as they speak out of their hearts you may be sure they intend to speak into ours. Nowhere else. As true music is made in some one's heart, we must feel it in our own hearts as we play it or it will mean nothing. The heart must make it warm, then the beauties of the music will come out. It is strange how our moods tell themselves. All we do with our eyes and with our ears, with the tongue and with the hands, what we do with our thoughts even, is sure to say of itself whether we are doing with a willing heart or not. It is curious that the truth will come out of whatever seems to be a secret, but curious as it may be, it does come out. We must think of that.

Every one of us knows the difference between doing willingly and unwillingly. We know that things done with joy and with eagerness are well done and seem to spring directly from the heart. Not only that, but they really inspire joy and eagerness in those who are about us. Inspire is just the word. Look it up in your dictionary and see that it means exactly what happens—to breathe into—they breathe joy and happiness into all things else, and it comes out of our hearts.

Now happiness can be told in many ways: in laughter, in the eyes, in a game, in a life like that of Polissena's, in anything, but in nothing that does not win the heart. As happiness can be shown in anything, it can be shown in music. We can put happiness into play, likewise we can put happiness into music. And as much of it as we put into anything will come out. Besides, we might just as well learn now as at another time, this: Whatever we put into what we do will come out. It may be happiness or idleness or hatred or courage; whatever goes into what we do comes out very plainly. Everything, remember. That means much. If you should practise for an hour, wishing all the time to be doing something else, you may be sure that your wish is coming out of your playing so plainly that every one knows it. Do you think that is strange? Well, it may be, but it is strictly true.

No one may be able to explain why and how, but certainly it is true that as we play our music all that goes on in the heart finds its way into the head, and the arms, and the hands, into the music, off through the air, and into the hearts of every one who is listening. So it is a valuable truth for us to remember, that whatever we put into our music will come out and we cannot stop it; and other people will get it, and know what we are by it.

Once we fully understand how music will show forth our inmost feelings we shall begin to understand its truthfulness and its power, as well as its beauty. We shall see from our first days that music will tell the truth. That will help us to understand a little the true mission of art, "either to state a true thing, or adorn a serviceable one."[7] The moment we understand this a very little we shall begin to love art. We shall be glad and willing for music to reveal us, to show the spirit within us, because little by little with the understanding will come love and reverence for the beautiful thoughts that are locked up in tones.

Men who want to tell something to very many people, many of whom they do not know and to whom they cannot go, write down all they have to say and make a book of it. There are some men, however, who have many beautiful thoughts which they wish to tell to those who can understand; these may dwell in their own land or in other lands; in their own time or in future time. But the message of these men is so beautiful and so delicate that it cannot be told in words, so they tell it in music. Then, in their own land and in other lands, in their own day and forever after, people can find out the delicate thoughts by studying the pages of the music, seeking with their hearts the thought that came out of the master's heart.

Do you wonder that composers revere their art? We are told of Chopin that art was for him a high and holy vocation.[8] Do you wonder? Let me read you a few words about his devotion: "In order to become a skilful and able master he studied, without dreaming of the ... fame he would obtain." "Nothing could be purer, more exalted, than his thoughts,"[9] because he knew that if his thoughts were not pure the impurity would come out in his music.

The music that has first been felt in the heart and then written down finds its way and tells all about the heart, where it was born. When you play and feel that you are playing from the heart, you may be sure you are on the right path. The beautiful thing is, that this is true no matter how simple music is. The very simplest will tell all about us. Remember, in playing music, that great and good men have put into tones thoughts which will be a joy and comfort to the world forever. Some one of these Talks will be about classic and common music. But even now I am sure we understand that good music comes from pure thought, and pure thought comes from a good heart. That, surely, is clear and simple.

Pure music is earnest and songful. It has meaning in every part. No tone is without a lofty purpose. That is true music. It is classic from the heart that is put into it.

By being faithful to our music it will do for us more than we can dream. Do you know the inscription that used to be over the north gate of the city of Siena, in Italy?

"Siena opens not only her gates, but her heart to you."

CHAPTER IV.

THE TONES ABOUT US

"Scientific education ought to teach us to see the invisible as well as the visible in nature."—John Tyndall [10]

There used to live in England a famous scientist named Tyndall, who was interested, among other things, in the study of sound. He studied sounds of all kinds, made experiments with them, wrote down what he observed, and out of it all he wrote a book,[11] useful to all who desire to learn about sound and its nature.

One day, Tyndall and a friend were walking up one of the mountains of the Alps.[12] As they ascended the path, Tyndall's attention was attracted by a shrill sound, which seemed to come from the ground at his feet. Being a trained thinker he was at once curious to know what was the cause of this. By looking carefully he found that it came from a myriad of small insects which swarmed by the side of the path. Having satisfied himself as to what it was he spoke to his companion about the shrill tone and was surprised to learn that he could not hear it. Tyndall's friend could hear all ordinary sound perfectly well. This, however, seemed to be sound of such a character as did not reach his sense of hearing. One who like Tyndall listened carefully to sounds of all kinds would quickly detect anything uncommon. This little incident teaches us that sounds may go on about us and yet we know nothing of them. Also it teaches us to think about tones, seek them, and in the first days increase our acquaintance and familiarity with them.

Men of science, who study the different ways in which the mind works, tell us that habit and also a busy mind frequently make us unconscious of many things about us. Sometimes we have not noticed the clock strike, although we have been in the room on the hour; or some one speaks to us, and because we are thinking of something else we fail to hear what is said to us. It certainly is true that very many people do not hear half of the sounds that go on about them, sounds which, if but heeded, would teach people a great deal. And of all people, those who study music should be particularly attentive to sounds of all kinds. Indeed, the only way to begin a music education is to begin by learning to listen. Robert Schumann, a German composer, once wrote a set of rules for young musicians. As it was Schumann's habit to write only what was absolutely needed we may be sure he regarded his rules as very important.

There are sixty-eight of them, and the very first has reference to taking particular notice of the tones about us. If we learn it from memory we shall understand it better and think of it oftener. Besides that, we shall have memorized the serious thought of a truly good and great man. This is what he says:

"The cultivation of the ear is of the greatest importance. Endeavor early to distinguish each tone and key. Find out the exact tone sounded by the bell, the glass, and the cuckoo."

There is certainly a good hint in this. Let us follow it day by day, and we shall see how many are the tones about us which we scarcely ever notice. We should frequently listen and find who of us can distinguish the greatest number of different sounds. Then we shall learn to listen attentively to sounds and noises. Bit by bit all sounds, especially beautiful ones, will take on a new and deeper meaning to us; they will be full of a previously unrecognized beauty which will teach us to love music more and more sincerely.

In order that we may better understand how sounds are related to each other we should learn early to sing the major scale so that it will go readily up and down as a melody. As we become more and more familiar with it we must think frequently of its separate tones so as to feel just how each one sounds in the scale, how it fits in the scale, and just what it says, in fact; we shall then notice after a while that we can hear the scale with the inner ear, which is finer and more delicate.[13]

We should have names for the scale-tones like the pretty Italian syllables, or, if not these, whatever our teacher suggests. Then we should have a conception of the tones as they are related. We should learn that every tone of the scale is colored by the tonic. Every one gets a character from the tonic which tells us all about it, because we learn to hear its relation to its principal tone. In a little while, with patience, we shall be able to hear the scale-tones in any order we may choose to think them. That power will be a fine help forever after—we must be sure to get it in the first days.

Whenever we hear two tones we should try to find them on the piano. This will make us listen more attentively to the tone sounded by the clock, the church-bell, the bird, the drinking-glass. And what a lot there are, like the squeaking door, the cricket, the noise of the wind and rain, the puff of the engine, and all the other sounds we hear in a day. Bit by bit, in this way, our familiarity with tones will grow and we shall be well repaid for all the trouble. Gradually we shall become better listeners—but about listening we are to speak in our next Talk. This, however, may be said now: Let us always be sure to listen with special care to two tones, calling one the tonic, or first, of the major scale and finding what degree the other is, or near what degree it lies. This will make us better acquainted with the scale and we shall learn that all the music we have comes out of it.

We must also listen to tones so that we can tell something about them besides their scale names. We must learn to describe tones, tell whether they are high or low, sweet or harsh, loud or soft, long or short. For instance, through the window I can hear a church-bell. Some one is ringing it slowly so that the tones are long. The tone is not a very high one (it is G above middle C) and the quality is rich and mellow. This describes the church-bell tone quite well, and in like manner we may describe all the sounds we hear. We should make it a habit often to stand or to sit perfectly still and to listen to everything that goes on about us. Even in the country, where all seems as quiet as possible, we shall be surprised at the great number of sounds.

There are some other tones to which I fear we are prone not to listen. I mean the tones which the piano makes when we play finger-exercises. We think perhaps of the finger motion, which is not all; or we think of nothing, which is very bad; or our thoughts begin to picture other things even while we play, which is the worst of all, and bit by bit we actually forget what we are doing. One of the quickest ways to become unable to hear sounds correctly is to play the piano without thinking fully of what we are doing. Therefore it must be a rule never to play a tone without listening acutely to it. If in the first days we determine to do this and remain faithful to it, we shall always touch the piano keys carefully, thoughtfully, and reverentially.

Elsewhere we shall have some definite tone lessons for the purpose of making us familiar with the tones about us. But no rule can exceed in importance this one, never to make any music unthinkingly.

By care and practice we soon become so skilful as to notice tones with the readiness we notice colors in the garden. The sense of tone must be as strong in us as is the sense of color. Then we shall be able to tell differences of tones which are nearly the same, as readily as we can now tell two varieties of yellow, for instance. A bit of perseverance in this and the beauties even of common sounds shall be revealed to us.

CHAPTER V.

LISTENING

"You must listen as if listening were your life."—Phillips Brooks [14]

In our last Talk we learned that it was quite possible for sounds to be about us and yet we not hear them. Sometimes, as in the case of Tyndall's companion, it is because we are not capable; at other times, as when the clock strikes and we do not hear, it is because we are occupied with other things. It is from this latter fact—being occupied with other things—that we can learn what listening is. Listening is not being occupied with other things. It is being completely attentive to what we are expected to hear.

The condition of being occupied with other thoughts when we should be listening is known as inattention. To listen with full attention, all other things being entirely absent from the mind, is one form of concentration.

Inattention is a destroyer. It divides our power between two or more things when it should be directed upon a single thing. Concentration gives us greater and greater mind-power. If you will look in the dictionary to find what concentration means (you should be good friends with the dictionary) you will find it is made up of con[15] meaning with, and centrum, a center, "with a center," or "to come to a center." If you hold a magnifying-glass between your hand and the sun you will find that at a certain distance the sunlight is in a circle. By changing the distance with delicacy you can diminish the circle to almost a point,—you make the light come to a center. When the circle of light is large, no particular effect is noted by the hand. When, however, the circle is as small as it can be made you feel a sensation of warmth which, if continued long enough, will really burn the hand. That small circle is the sunlight in concentration. The rays of sunlight, instead of being scattered, are centered. They burn the hand because they are full of power—powerful.

By way of example: Let the different rays stand for inattention and the tiny circle of light for concentration. The former has little or no power; the latter is full of power. This very well illustrates what happens, both when our thoughts are scattered over a large area, and when they are brought together—concentrated—in a small circle. The first listening indeed which should claim our attention is not tone-listening, but listening to what is said to us. No one under a good teacher ever learns well who is not attentive and obedient. And then listening and doing are inseparably joined. Tone-listening makes us self-critical and observant, and we are assured by men of science that unless we become good observers in our early years, it is later impossible for us.[16]

In the previous Talk we spoke about listening to all kinds of sounds, particularly those out-of-doors. In this Talk we shall speak only of real music-listening. You know, now, that music born out of the heart is the thought of a good man. Of course, beautiful thoughts of any kind should be listened to not only with attention, but with reverence. Reverence is the tribute which the thoughtful listener pays to the music of a man who has expressed himself beautifully in tone. This at once reveals to us that we should listen to what is great for the purpose of getting ideals. We hear what we hope to attain. It is said of the violinist, Pierre Baillot, that when only ten years of age he heard the playing of Viotti, and though he did not hear it again for twenty years the performance ever remained in his mind as an ideal to be realized in his studies, and he worked to attain it.

The pupils of the great Viennese teacher of the piano, Theodor Leschetizky, say he asks no question more frequently than "Can you not hear?" It is not only difficult to listen to ourselves, but listening is one thing and decidedly a superior thing, while hearing is another and equally inferior thing. And it shows us, when we think of it, that no self-criticism is possible until we forget all things else and listen to what we are doing and listen with concentration. It now becomes clear to us that no one becomes an intelligent musician who is not skilled in tone sense, in listening, and having thoughts about what is heard.

We may read again from the excellent rules of Robert Schumann:

"Frequently sing in choruses, especially the middle parts; this will help to make you musical."

Out of this we learn to try to hear more than the melody, to try sometimes not to think of the melody, but to listen only to that which accompanies it. When, in school, you sing in two and three parts, notice how one is inclined always to sing the soprano. The melody pulls us away from another part if we are not concentrated upon our part. Yet notice how beautifully musical the lower parts are. Listen intently to them whatever part you sing.

It seems in music that we learn to listen in two directions. First, by training the attention merely to follow prominent sounds and to be conscious of all of them; then, later, we do not need to think so much of the prominent melody but we strive to hear the accompanying parts. These are the melodies which are somewhat concealed by the principal one; not truly concealed either, for they are plain enough if we will listen. They make one think of flowers hidden in the grass and foliage. They are none the less beautiful though they are concealed; for the sunlight seeks them out and makes them blossom.

We find hidden melodies in all good music because it is the character of good music to have interesting and beautiful melodic thought everywhere. There are never meaningless tones allowed. Every sound says something and is needed. It is curious that in our playing the moment we put our thoughts upon any tone or voice part with the desire to hear it, it comes out at once as plainly as if it was the highest melody. That illustrates the power of thought concentrated upon even a hidden thing. You know how in Bach even the piano works move as if all parts were to be sung by voices. It reminds one of conversation; of the story, of the question and answer, of the merry chat in a pleasant company. Some bits of sentence are tripping and full of laughter,[17] others grave and majestic,[18] others have wonderful dignity of heart and mind.[19]

Such qualities give music interest and meaning in every part. It will not take you long to discover that it is just the absence of these qualities that makes other music common.

The melody is not sustained by anything particularly well worth listening to. One might say that good music is like the foliage of the garden, every leaf and petal variously yet finely formed, and all combined to make a beautiful whole.

When you have learned carefully to follow the accompaniment of a melody, try to follow the single voice parts in the chorus, particularly the Bass, Tenor, and Alto. And when you go to orchestral concerts learn early to follow special instruments like the clarinet, the oboe, the drum.

Especially try to follow the lower strings, the viola, the 'cello, and the bass. They are strongly characteristic. You will learn their peculiar qualities only by giving them special and concentrated thought. You will now see that acute and careful listening has its definite ways and purposes. Here they are:

I. Listening comes from concentration.

II. When listening to great music it must be with reverence as well as with attention.

III. We must listen for ideals.

IV. We must listen in order to be self-critical.

V. Constant listening to true music reveals that there is never a tone used unless it has a meaning.

And besides all this we must think that among those who listen to us there may be some one who has learned this careful concentrated way. Then we shall have it ever in mind to "play as if in the presence of a master."[20]

CHAPTER VI.

THINKING IN TONE

"The gods for labor sell us all good things."—Epicharmus [21]

Perhaps you have some doubt as to exactly what is meant by music-thinking. Being somewhat acquainted with composers and with music, the thought may here come to you that all the music we hear in the world must have been made by somebody—by many somebodies, in fact. They have had to sit down, and forgetting all things else, listen intently to the music-thought which fills the mind. If you will sit quietly by yourself you will discover that you can easily think words and sentences and really hear them in the mind without pronouncing anything. In quite the same way the composer sits and hears music, tone by tone, and as clearly as if it were played by a piano or an orchestra. And to him the tones have a clear meaning, just as words have a clear meaning to us. Naturally, one can see that there could be no other way. Unless the composer can think out everything exactly there could be no music, for music must be written, and one can only write what one thinks. So at this point the thought to remember is this: Music must exist in some one's mind before others can have it to hear and enjoy.

In like manner—just the same manner, in fact—the painter is one who thinks pictures; the sculptor, one who thinks statues; the architect, one who thinks buildings. They think these things just as you think words; and as you tell your thoughts in spoken words, so they tell their thoughts in printed music, in painted pictures, in chiseled statues, and in erected buildings. Now, from all this it should be clear to you that there can be nothing which has not first been thought of by some one. You think the door must be closed and you close it; you think you must know the time and you look at the clock; you think the one hand should play more loudly than the other and you try to do it.

Power to get things and to do things comes to us rapidly only in the fairy-tales. In the real, beautiful, healthy world in which we live we have to work hard and honestly for the power either to get things or to do things. By faithful labor must we win what we want. What we do not labor for we do not get. That is a condition of things so simple that a child can readily understand it. But all, children and their elders, are apt to forget it. In the life of every great man there is a story different from that of every other great man, but in every one of them this truth about laboring for the power one has is found.

In our Talk on Listening, it was said that the sounds we hear around us are the more easily understood if we first become familiar with the melody which is called the major scale. But in order to think music it is necessary to know it—in fact, music-thinking is impossible without it. As it is no trouble to learn the scale, all of you should get it fixed in the mind quickly and securely.

It is now possible for you to hear the scale without singing its tones aloud. Listen and see if that is not so! Now think of the melodies you know, the songs you sing, the pieces you play. You can sing them quite loudly (can you sing them?) or in a medium tone, or you can hum them softly as if to yourself; or further yet, you can think them without making the faintest sound, and every tone will be as plain as when you sang it the loudest. Here, I can tell you that Beethoven wrote many of his greatest works when he was so deaf that he could not hear the music he made. Hence, he must have been able to write it out of his thought just as he wanted it to sound. When you understand these steps and ways you will then know about the beginning of music-thinking.

Let us inquire in this Talk what the piano has to do in our music-thinking. What relation is there between the music in the mind and the tones produced by the piano? It seems really as if the piano were a photographic camera, making for us a picture of what we have written,—a camera so subtle indeed, that it pictures not things we can see and touch, but invisible things which exist only within us. But faithful as the piano is in this, it may become the means of doing us much injury. We may get into the habit of trusting the piano to think for us, of making it do so, in fact. Instead of looking carefully through the pages of our new music, reading and understanding it with the mind, we run to the piano and with such playing-skill as we have we sit down and use our hands instead of our minds. Now a great many do that, young and old. But the only people who have a chance to conceive their music rightly are the young; the old, if they have not already learned to do it, never can. That is a law which cannot be changed.

We have talked about listening so much that it should now be a settled habit in us. If it is we are learning every day a little about tones, their qualities and character. And we do this not alone by hearing the tones, but by giving great heed to them. Let us now remember this: listening is not of the ears but of the thoughts. It is thought concentrated upon hearing. The more this habit of tone-listening goes on in us, the more power we shall get out of our ability to read music. All these things help one another. We shall soon begin to discover that we not only have thoughts about sounding-tones, but about printed tones. This comes more as our knowledge of the scale increases.

We can now learn one of the greatest and one of the most wonderful truths of science: Great knowledge of anything comes from never ceasing to study the first steps.

The major scale, as we first learn it, seems a perfectly simple thing. But if we think of it all our lives we shall never discover the wonders there are in it. Hence, three simple rules for us to follow in learning to think music are these:

1. To listen to all tones.

2. Never to stop studying the major scale.

3. To become accustomed to hear tones within.

If we are faithful to these we shall, with increasing study and industry, become more and more independent of the piano. We shall never think with our hands, nor depend upon anything outside of ourselves for the meaning contained in printed tone-thought.

If now we join two things we shall get the strength of both united, which is greater than of either alone.

If in our playing lessons we have only the very purest music (heart music, remember), and if we are faithful in our simpler thinking lessons, we shall gain the power not only of pure thought, but of stronger and stronger thought. This comes of being daily in the presence of great thoughts—for we are in the presence of great thoughts when we study great music, or read a great poem, or look at a great picture, or at a great building. All these things are but signs made manifest,—that is to say, made plain to us—of the pure thought of their makers.

Thomas Carlyle, a Scotch author of this century, spoke very truly when he said:

"Great men are profitable company; we cannot look upon a great man without gaining something by him."[22]

CHAPTER VII.

WHAT WE SEE AND HEAR

"You must feel the mountains above you while you work upon your little garden."—Phillips Brooks [23]

Somewhere else we shall have some definite lessons in music-thinking. Let us then devote this Talk to finding out what is suggested to us by the things we see and hear.

Once a boy wrote down little songs. When the people asked him how he could do it, he replied by saying that he made his songs from thoughts which most other people let slip. We have already talked about thought and about learning to express it. If a person of pure thought will only store it up and become able to express it properly, when the time comes he can make little songs or many other things; for all things are made of thought. The poem is stored-up thought expressed in words; the great cathedral like the one at Winchester, in England, or the one near the Rhine, at Cologne, in Germany, is stored-up thought expressed in stone. So with the picture and the statue: they are stored-up thought on canvas and in marble.[24] In short, we learn by looking at great things just what the little ones are; and we know from poems and buildings and the like, that these, and even commoner things, like a well-kept garden, a tidy room, a carefully learned lesson, even a smile on one's face result, every one of them, from stored-up thought.

We can consequently make a definition of THINGS by saying they are what is thought. Things are made of thought. Even if you cannot understand this fully now, keep it by you and as you grow older its truth will be more and more clear. It will be luminous. Luminous is just the word, for it comes from a word in another language and means light. Now the better you understand things the more light you have about them. And out of this you can understand how well ignorance has been compared with darkness. Hence, from the poem, the building, the painting, the statue, and from commoner things we can learn, as it was said in a previous Talk, that music is stored-up thought told in beautiful tones.

Now let us heed the valuable part of all this. If poems, statues, and all other beautiful things are made out of stored-up thought (and commoner things are, too), we ought to be able, by studying the things, to tell what kind of a person it was who thought them; or, in other words, who made them. It is true, we can. We can tell all the person's thought, so far as his art and principal work are concerned. Nearly all his life is displayed in the works he makes. We can tell the nature of the man, the amount of study he has done, but best of all we can tell his meaning. The face tells all its past history to one who knows how to look.[25] His intentions are everywhere as plain as can be in what he does.

Thus you see there is more in a person's work than what we see at the first glance. There are reflections in it as plain as those in a mountain lake. And as the mountain lake reflects only what is above it, so the work of the musician, of the artist, of any one in fact, reflects those thoughts which forever hover above the others. Thoughts of good, thoughts of evil, thoughts of generosity, thoughts of selfish vanity, these, and every other kind, are so strongly reflected in the work we do that they are often more plainly seen than the work itself. And with the works of a great artist before us we may find out not only what he did and what he knew, but what he felt and even what he did not want to say.

We now know what music-thinking is. Also, we see why the young musician needs to learn to think music. Really, he is not a musician until he can think correctly in tone. And further than this, when we have some understanding of music-thought we not only think about what we play and hear, but we begin to inquire what story it tells and what meaning it should convey. We begin to seek in music for the thought and intention of the composer, and, little by little, even before we know it, we begin to seek out what kind of mind and heart the composer had. We begin really to study his character from the works he has left us.

We have now taken the first really intelligent step toward knowing for ourselves something about common and classic music. Later on, as our ability increases, this will be of great value to us. We begin to see, bit by bit, what the author intended. That is the real test of it all. We do not want to find mere jingle in music, we want music that says something. Even a very young child knows that "eenty meenty meiny moe" is not real sense, though it is a pleasant string of sounds to say in a game.

Thus we learn to look into what we hear and into what we see and try to find how much thought there is in it, and the kind of thought it is. We want to know if goodness is expressed; if the best work of the man is before us, or if, for a lower reason, his selfishness and vanity are most prominent. And let us remember that as we seek these things in the works of others, so others of thoughtful kind will watch our doings, our playing, our speech, our little habits, and all to see what our intentions are each time we express ourselves. They will look to see what thoughts we are putting into our doings, whether thoughts of goodness or of selfishness. And our actions will always be just as good as the thought we put into them.

Now a great and a common mistake is, that sometimes we hope by some mysterious change, as in a fairy tale, that they will be better than what we intend. But in the first days let us learn that this is not possible.

CHAPTER VIII.

THE CLASSICS.[26]

"Genuine work done faithfully, that is eternal."—Thomas Carlyle

The older we grow and the more we study, the more we shall hear about the classics, about classic music, and classic art, and classic books. From the beginning let us keep it in our minds that one of our duties is to find out the difference between what is classic and what is not. Then we shall have a proper understanding. An English writer on art says: "The writers and painters of the classic school set down nothing but what is known to be true, and set it down in the perfectest manner possible in their way."[27]

And we have already learned that thought from the heart, expressed in tones, is good music. On the other hand, a thought with the heart not in it, expressed in tone, makes poor or common music. Mendelssohn wrote in one of his letters: "When I have composed a piece just as it springs from my heart, then I have done my duty toward it."[28] But in writing thoughts, whether in words or in tones, there is a very important thing to add to the bidding of the heart. It is the training of the mind. With both of these one works and judges wisely.

With thought and intention ever so pure, but with no education, one would not be able to write for others, and with a little education one would be able to write only in a partially correct way. This brings us to one of the most interesting Talks we shall have. Let us try to make it clear and simple.

We can easily imagine a man both true and good who can neither write nor spell. Happily, in these days, nearly all people who are old enough know how to do both. We can understand that this man may have beautiful thoughts—the thoughts of a true poet or of a true artist—but being unable to write or to spell he could not put his thoughts on paper for others to read and to study. This is the way thoughts are preserved and made into books so that people may benefit by them.

It would, therefore, be necessary for this man, about whom we speak, to get the assistance of some one who knew how to write thoughts and to spell their words. Then, together, they would have to talk about the thoughts, choose proper words, form the sentences, and make all fit rightly together as a writer must who desires to be clear. But it is more than likely that the one who writes would not do all these things to the satisfaction of the other. Of this there could be but one result. The person who had the beautiful thoughts would be forever wishing that he had learned in the first days to write and to spell. Then he could do all these things for himself and show his thoughts to others exactly as he wished them to appear.

Now it is clear that some may have beautiful and valuable thoughts and not know how to write them, while others may have the ability to write without having thoughts worth preserving. Evidently what one must have are both beautiful thoughts and ability to write them.

Did you think when I read you that bit from the letter of Mendelssohn that all a composer has to do is to find in his heart just what he wants to say? As we have already discovered, that is not enough. To show you that Mendelssohn was not afraid of hard work let us read a little from another of his letters.[29] Mendelssohn had resolved to work in Germany and maintain himself. "If I find that I cannot do this, then I must leave it for London or Paris, where it is easier to get on. I see indeed where I should be more honored, and live more gaily and more at my ease than in Germany, where a man must press forward, and toil, and take no rest,—still, if I can succeed there, I prefer the latter."[30]

We can now understand that it is quite the same with word-thinkers and with tone-thinkers. Good thoughts and the proper writing of them make the classics.

Out of this thought there comes another. It is this: Great thoughts, expressed well, out of a great heart, make the works which last the longest; and still further, for one truth leads out of another. Only they can appreciate the classics who have something that is classic within them. They must have the heart true in its feeling, tender in its sentiments. Even a child can have that. They must have the mind trained in the truest and best way of expressing thought. And a child may begin to learn that. Hence we see that a child may be classic worthy. Only we must never, never, no matter what is our ability, think we are better or above others. The more talents one has the more one is expected to do and the greater duty it is.[31]

Thus far we have three truths; now here is a fourth: Some love the classics sooner and better than others because they have more power. And how do they get it? They think more (thought-making); they feel more (heart-learning); and they see more (truth-seeking).

Let us at once go back and gather together these four truths. They are important. Perhaps some of us who are willing to spend the time will learn them from memory.

And to repay us for the trouble of doing it we shall have greater and greater understanding of many things. Here they are:

I. Good thoughts and the proper writing of them make the classics.

II. Great thoughts, expressed well, out of a great heart, make the works which last the longest.

III. Only they can appreciate the classics who have something that is classic within them.

IV. Some love the classics sooner and better than others because they have more power.

What shall these truths teach us? That true music cannot be learned rapidly; that the way of Art is long and difficult. But if the way is long, it is yet beautiful in every turn; if it is difficult, it is yet worth a struggle for what comes. As you read the lives of the great composers you will learn that they went willingly about their tasks, doing each one well. This is done by all great men. Great men take short steps carefully, no matter how rapidly they can go.

One of them [32] wrote: "Success comes with tiny steps." And it comes entirely unsought. Besides all this we are to remember that the power for these things comes from

I. Thought-making;

II. Heart-learning;

III. Truth-seeking.

Now, just to end with let us read a few words from a book I trust we all may read some day: [33] "Great art is the expression of the mind of a great man, and mean art of a weak man." Let us remember that in choosing things to play.

Further on Ruskin says: "If stone work is well put together, it means that a thoughtful man planned it, and a careful man cut it, and an honest man cemented it." [34]

Likewise in these things one can see what is classic—work out of the heart and well done, and that comes from a thoughtful, careful, honest person.

CHAPTER IX.

WHAT WE SHOULD PLAY.

"But blessings do not fall in listless hands."—Bayard Taylor.

We already begin to understand what the classics are. Year by year as our interest in the beautiful increases, we shall gain more definite knowledge about classic art. That which is classic will begin to announce itself in us. Our own choice indicates our taste but does not always indicate what is best for us. And one of the purposes of art is to improve the taste by setting before us the finest works; in these, by study, we find beauty with which we are unacquainted. Thus we enlarge our capacity for it.

Because we are born with taste unformed and untrained you can at once see the reason for gradually increasing the tasks. They are always a little more difficult—like going up a mountain—but they give a finer and finer view. The outlook from the mountain-top cannot be had all at once. We must work our way upward for it. Hence you will observe in your lessons that what was once a fitting task is no longer of quite the same value because of your increased power. But about this especially we shall have a Talk later on.

When one has heard much music of all kinds, one soon begins to understand that there are two kinds commonly chosen. Some players choose true music with pure thought in it, and do their best to play it well after the manner called for by the composer. Their aim is to give truthful expression to the music of a good writer. Other players seem to work from a motive entirely different. They select music which is of a showy character, with much brilliancy and little thought in it. Their aim is not to show what good music is, but to show themselves. The desire of the first is truth, of the second is vanity.

Now, as we examine into this, and into both kinds of music, we discover much. It proves that we must work for the best; for the truthful music, not for the vain music. As we get better acquainted with true music we find it more and more interesting—it keeps saying new things to us. We go to it again and again, getting new meanings. But the showy music soon yields all it has; we find little or nothing more in it than at first. As it was made not from good thought but for display, we cannot find newer and more beautiful thought in it, and the display soon grows tiresome. True music is like the light in a beautifully-cut gem, it seems that we never see all it is—it is never twice the same; always a new radiance comes from it because it is a true gem through and through. It is full of true light, and true light is always opposed to darkness; and darkness is the source of ignorance.

From all this you can now understand the quaintly-expressed opinion of a very wise man, who said: "In discharge of thy place, set before thee the best example."[35] That means whatever we strive to learn should be learned from works of the best kind. In the beginning, we cannot choose wisely the best examples to set before ourselves; therefore it is for us to heed what another wise man said: "As to choice in the study of pieces, ask the advice of more experienced persons than yourself; by so doing you will save much time." [36] You thereby save time doubly. Later on in your life you will have no bad taste to overcome—that is one saving; and already you know from childhood many classics, and that is another saving. What we learn in childhood is a power all our lives.

You can see plainly, now, that both in the choice of pieces and in the manner of playing them, a person's character will come out. We saw in the last Talk how character has to come out in writing. Only a very common character would select pieces written entirely for a vain show—of rapid runs, glittering arpeggios, and loud, unmeaning chords. Worse than that, such a choice of pieces displays two common people,—three, in fact: A composer who did not write pure thought from the heart; a teacher who did not instil good thoughts into the pupil's heart; and yourself (if really you care for such things) who play from a vain desire to be considered brilliant.

A player who devotes the mind and the hands only to what a meaningless composer writes for them is not worthy of any power. With our hands in music, as with the tongue in speech, let us strive from the beginning to be truthful. Let us try in both ways to express the highest truth we are able to conceive. Then in art we shall, at least, approach near unto the true artist; and in life we shall approach near unto the true life. Every mere empty display-piece we study takes up the time and the opportunity wherein we could learn a good composition, by a master of the heart. And it is only with such music that you will, during your life, get into the hearts of those who are most worthy for you to know. Out of just this thought Schumann has two rules now very easy for us to understand:

"Never help to circulate bad compositions; on the contrary, help to suppress them with earnestness."

"You should neither play bad compositions, nor, unless compelled, listen to them."

We now come to a really definite conclusion about the compositions we should play and to an extent as to how we should play them.

The heart, the mind, and the hands, or the voice, if you sing, should unite in our music; and be consecrated to the beautiful. Consecrate is just exactly the word. Look for it in your dictionary.[37] It comes from two other words, does it not? Con meaning with and sacer meaning holiness. Thus devote heart and head and hands with holiness to the beautiful. This is very clear, I am sure.

It is also worth doing. "With holiness" describes how to play and really what to play. A composition which has been born of a true man is in thought already consecrated. He has heard it and felt it within himself. Daily you must get closer and closer to these messages and meanings. And are they not already more luminous to you? And do you remember what we said luminous means?

CHAPTER X.

THE LESSON.

"All people value most what has cost them much labor."

—Aristotle.[38]

It is true that music is beautiful and that it gives us happiness and comfort. But, nevertheless, music is hard to learn for every one; harder for some than for others, but hard for all. It is well and best that it should be so. We appreciate most highly that which we labor for earnestly. Just imagine if every one could sing or play merely by wishing it! Then music would be so common and so much the talent of all that it would cease to give us joy. Why? Because one gained it by a wish. That is not enough. From this can we learn to understand the great secret of it all? I think we can. Let us see! The secret is this: Music is a joy because it takes us out of ourselves and we work hard to get it. Music teaches us what a wonderful power there is within us, if we will only strive to bring it out. Education is good for us for this same reason. As you learn more and more about words, you will see more in this word Education.

It means to lead out what is within us. To lead music out of the heart becomes the object, then, of your lessons. One cannot drive music into you; it must be led out.

Where shall we look for music that it may be led out? Only in the heart. That is where all is in every one of us. But often in our hearts there is so much else, so much vanity, self-love, conceit, love for other things, that the music is almost beyond reach. Almost, but never entirely. In the heart of every one is music. But often it is deep, deep down, covered by these other things. The older we grow and the more other things we see and think about, the deeper and deeper down does the music get.

It is like heaping rocks, and dirt, and sticks on a bubbling spring. The spring is down there, bubbling freely beneath it all, still striving to be as free and as songful as before; but it cannot. People may come and go, may pass near to it, and hear not one of its sounds; they may never suspect that there is such a thing ready to go on merrily if it could.

When is the best time to lead water out of the spring, and music out of the heart? Before other things begin to cover it. With music the best time is in the early days, in childhood time—in the first days. We shall hear those words many times. Then little by little the bubbling spring of melody gains its independence; then, even if other things do come in, they cannot bury the music out of sight. The spring has been led forth and has grown stronger.

Thoughtful people who have suffered in learning—all people suffer in learning, thoughtful ones the most—wonder how they can make the task less painful for others. It will always cause us sorrow as well as joy to learn, and many people spend their lives in trying to have as little sorrow as possible come with the learning of the young. When such people are true and good and thoughtful and have infinite kindness, they are teachers; and the teachers impose tasks upon us severely, perhaps, but with kind severity. They study us and music, and they seek out the work each one of us must perform in order that we may keep the heart-springs pure and uncovered. Further than this, they find the way by which we shall lead the waters of life which flow out of the heart-springs. They find the way whither they should flow best.

Often in the doing of these things we find the lessons hard and wearisome, infinitely hard to bear, difficult, and not attractive. We wonder why all these things should be so, and we learn in the moment we ask that question that these painful tasks are the price we are paying for the development of our talent. That is truly the purpose of a lesson. And the dear teacher, wise because she has been painfully over the road herself, knows how good and necessary it is for us to labor as she directs.

Let us suppose you play the piano. There will be two kinds of lessons—one will be for the fingers, one for the mind. But really the mind also guides the finger-work; and the heart must be in all. Your exercises will give you greater power to speak with the fingers. Every new finger-exercise in piano-playing is like a new word in language. Provided with it, you can say more than you could before. The work for the mind is the classics. These are compositions by the greater and lesser masters with which you form the taste, while the technical exercises are provided to give you the power, the ability, to play them. Thus you see how well these two things go together.

Year after year, if you go on patiently, you will add to each of these tasks; more power will come to the fingers and to the mind. All this time you will be coming nearer and nearer to the true music. More and more will be coming out of your heart. The spring will not only continue to bubble clearly but it will become more powerful. Nothing is so wonderful as that.

Do you know what a sad thing it was for the man not to increase that one talent which had been given to him? [39] Perchance you have also one. Then find it, love it, increase it. Know that every step of the way, every bit of task, every moment of faith is paid for in later years ten thousandfold.

If now we remember our Talk on Listening it will serve us. Did we not say then that the first duty of a listener is to the one who speaks for his good? Lesson time is an opportunity above nearly all others when we should listen with love in our attention. Yes, nothing less than that, because—how many times we have heard it already—putting love into anything, is putting the heart into it, and with less than that we do not get all we may have.

This Talk, then, is important, because it gathers together many things that have gone before, and hints at some to come. Let us give the last words to speaking about that. A lesson suggests listening; listening suggests the teacher, who with infinite kindness and severity guides us; and the teacher suggests the beautiful road along which we go and what we hear as we travel, that is the music of the heart; and the music of the heart has in it the tones about us, and the greater and lesser masters who thought them into beautiful forms. The masters are as servants unto whom there is given to some one talent, to others two, and four, and more, but to each according to his worth, to be guided and employed in truth and honor; increased by each in accordance to his strength.

CHAPTER XI.

THE LIGHT ON THE PATH

"Let us seek service and be helpers of one another."

"Master," said the little child, "I am unhappy. Though I have companions and games, they do not content me. Even the music which I love above all the rest is not truly in my heart; nor is it the pleasure to me which it should be. What am I to do?"

And the master replied:

"There is a task, the greatest and severest of all. But a child must learn it. Thou must know from the first days, that all thou doest and sayest, whither thou goest, what thou seekest; these, all these, come from within. All that is seen of thee is of thy inner life. All thy doings, thy goings and comings, thy ways and thy desires, these are from within. And when all these things are for thyself there is misery.

"Now there are many things which may not be had by directly seeking them; of these the greatest are two. The one is that which already has given thee sadness in the heart,—the Light of the Face. And the other is happiness.

"But there is a way in which these are to be found. Dost thou not know that often, even with much trouble, thou canst not please thyself? But always, with little trouble or none, thou canst please another.

"And the way is Service.

"Thou poor little one! Thou hast come with thy complaint of unhappiness; and yet thou hast all that is bright and rare; companions, and music, and a dear home. Dost thou know that there are in the world uncounted poor ones, children like thyself, who have not their daily bread? And yet there are many of them who never fail to say: 'Lead us not into temptation.' And they say this without having tasted of the daily bread for which they have been taught to pray.

"And thou? Thou art unhappy. And thy daily bread is set before thee with music and with sunshine.

"Yet there are little ones, like thyself, who are hungry in the darkness.

"And thou? Thou art unhappy."

CHAPTER XII.

THE GREATER MASTERS

"In spite of all, I have never interrupted the study of music." —Palestrina

An opera writer of Italy, named Giovanni Pacini, once said that to study the writings of Mozart, Haydn, and Beethoven "lightens the mind of a student, since the classics are a continuous development of the most beautiful and simple melodies," and we sometimes hear it said that great men are they who dare to be simple. In our Talks thus far we have learned one important fact, which is, that music is truth expressed out of the heart. Of course we know that to be in the heart it must be felt, and to be expressed we must know a great deal about writing. Now we are able to imagine quite well what a great master is in music. As Pacini says, his melodies will be simple and beautiful, and as we ourselves know, his simple melodies will be an expression of truth out of the heart.

But to go only as far as this would not be enough. Many can write simply and well, and truthfully, yet not as a master. There must be something else. When we have found out what that something else is we shall understand the masters better and honor them more.

Everywhere in the history of music we read of what men have been willing to do for the love of their art. It is not that they have been willing to do when told; but that they have cheerfully done painful, laborious tasks of their own accord. The name of every master will recall great labor willingly given for music and equally great suffering willingly endured, nay, even sought out, that the music might be purer to them. Poor Palestrina went along many years through life with the scantiest means. But, as he says, "in spite of all, I have never interrupted the study of music." Bach was as simple and loyal a citizen as any land could have, and from the early years when he was a fatherless boy to the days of his sad affliction, he sacrificed always. Think of the miles he walked to hear Buxterhude, the organist; and in the earlier years, when he lived with Johann Christopher, his brother, how eagerly he sought learning in the art that so fascinated him. It was a constant willingness to learn honestly that distinguished him.

Any of us who will labor faithfully with the talents we have can do a great deal—more than we would believe. Even Bach himself said to a pupil: "If thou art equally diligent thou wilt succeed as I have."[40] He recognized that it matters little how much we wish for things to be as we want them; unless our wish-thoughts are forced into prompt action we cannot succeed; for while all thoughts seek action, wish-thoughts demand the most labor.

It would be pleasant to have a Talk about every one of the great masters to see in what particular way each of them sacrificed for the art he loved. In all of them the true qualities come out: in one as earnestness; in another as determination; in another as patriotism; but all are loyal to the art itself. It must be a very plain lesson to us to see that when men are willing to give all their thoughts to a subject they get much from it. And is it not quite as plain to see that no one can get much if he gives but a few unwilling minutes to it? I trust none who hear these Talks will ever think that with a little time given to their music, and that not freely given, they can ever get either pleasure or comfort from it. They never can. And rather than do it so they would better leave it undone. If we set out on the way to go to the masters we shall get there only by earnestness. Lagging is a disgrace to the one who travels and to the one to whom we go. It shows his laziness on the one hand, and his misunderstanding of the master on the other; for if he understood he would take no listless step.

Now we have said again and again that true music comes from the heart, and is simple. At the same time we find it difficult to understand the music of the masters. That is, some of us find it so. It seems anything but simple to us; and naturally we conclude that there is something wrong somewhere. We sit at our tasks, poring over the music, and we grow discouraged because we cannot play it. To think it a very hard task is natural, and we cannot bear to hear such tones. Well, let us not get discouraged for that; let us see!

First of all, the playing is more difficult to do than the music is to understand. Once a great master of the piano played to a lady who had never heard a great master before, and the playing was like beautiful lace. When it was over and the master had gone away, some one asked the lady how he had played, and she said:

"He played so that the music sounded as I thought it should."

And they asked her what she meant.

"Always I have been taught," she said, "to listen to music and to think it. I have been taught this more than I have been taught to play. And the music of the master-composers I always think of as beautiful and simple but hard to make it sound as it should. Often I have heard others say that the music of the masters is dull, and not beautiful, but that is really not what the people feel. It is difficult for them to play the music rightly. And again they cannot understand this: that art is often simple in, its truth, while those who look upon it are not! simple-hearted, as they regard it. This is hard to understand, but it is the true reason."

Now, if we think of what this cultured lady said, we shall think her wise. Whatever stumbling we may do with our fingers, let us still keep in our minds the purity of the music itself. This will in a sense teach us to regard reverentially the men who, from early years, have added beauties to art for us to enjoy to-day. The wisest of the Greeks [41] said:

"The treasures of the wise men of old, which they have left written in books, I turn over and peruse in company with my friends, and if we find anything good in them, we remark it, and think it a great gain, if we thus become more attracted to one another."

Once an English lady[42] wrote about a verse-writer: "No poet ever clothed so few ideas in so many words." Just opposite to this is a true poet, he who clothes in few words many and noble ideas. A master tells his message in close-set language.

Now, in the last minutes, let us see what a great master is:

I. He will be one who tells a beautiful message simply.

II. He has been willing to sacrifice and suffer for his art.

III. He has lived his every day in the simple desire to know his own heart better.

IV. Always he has concentrated his message into as few tones as possible, and his music, therefore, becomes filled to overflowing with meaning.

About the meaning of the masters, one of them has written this: "Whenever you open the music of Bach, Mozart, or Beethoven, its meaning comes forth to you in a thousand different ways." That is because thousands of different messages from the heart have been concentrated in it.

CHAPTER XIII.

THE LESSER MASTERS

"And the soul of a child came into him again."—I Kings, XVII: 22.

If, one day, some one should say to you, earnestly: "Well day are to you!" you would scarcely know what to make of it. You would at once understand that the person had knowledge of words but could not put them together rightly. And if the person continued to talk to you in this manner you might feel inclined to lose your patience and not listen. But if you would stop and consider things and examine yourself you would learn something well worth thinking about.

You would discover that your own ability to put words in the right order has come from being obedient. First of all, you have been willing to imitate what others said until you have thereby learned to speak quite well. Besides that, you have been corrected many times by those about you at home, and in school, until language is at length a careful habit in you. Every one knows at once what you mean. You see, therefore, that you may combine words in such a manner that you will be easily comprehended by others; or, as in the case of the imaginary person we began with, they may be combined in a perfectly senseless way. Consequently, it is not enough to know words alone, we must know what to do with them. The true art of using words is to put full and clear meaning into a few of them; to say as much as possible with as few words as you may select.

Tones may be treated in the same manner as words. One can write tones in such a manner as to say quite as senseless a thing as "Well day are to you!" Many do. This teaches you that true and simple tone-sentences, like similar word-sentences, must have for their object to say the fullest and clearest meaning in as little space as possible.

For many hundreds of years thoughtful composers have studied about this. They have tried in every way to discover the secrets underlying tone-writing so that the utmost meaning should come out when they are united. Tones thus arranged according to the laws of music-writing make sense. To learn this art all great composers have studied untiringly. They have recognized the difficulty of putting much meaning in little space, and to gain this ability they have found no labor to be too severe.

We must remember that there is no end of music in the world which was not written by the few men whom we usually call the great composers. Perhaps you will be interested to know about these works. Many of them are really good—your favorite pieces, no doubt. When we think of it, it is with composers as with trees of the forest. Great and small, strong and weak, grow together for the many purposes for which they are created. They could not all be either great or small. There must be many kinds; then the young in time take the place of the old, and the strong survive the weak. Together beneath the same sky, deep-rooted in the beautiful, bountiful earth, they grow side by side. The same sun shines upon them all, the same wind and the same rain come to them, selecting no one before another. What are they all doing? Each living its true life, as best it can. It is true they may not come and go, they may not choose, but as we see them, beautiful in their leaves and branches we feel the good purpose to which they live and, unconsciously, perhaps, we love them.

Among us it is quite the same. Some are more skilful than others. But be our skill great or small, we are not truly using it until we have devoted it to a worthy purpose. And as with us, so it is with the musicians. There are the great and small. The great ones—leaders of thought—we call the great masters. The lesser are earnest men, who have not as much power as the masters, but they are faithful in small things.

They sing lesser songs it is true, but not less beautiful ones. Often these lesser ones think more as we do. They think simply and about the things which we have often in our minds. It is such thoughts as these which we have in our best moments that we love so much when we see them well expressed by one who is a good and delicate writer, either of tones or words. Particularly do we understand these thoughts well in the first years of our music when nearly all the works of the greater composers are above us.

Thus are the many composers (who yet are not great masters) of value to us because they write well a kind of thought which is pure and full of meaning, and which we can understand. They give us true pleasure day after day in the beginning and seem at the same time to help us onward to the ability of understanding the great masters. This they do by giving our thought training in the right direction.

Now, we know that the very best music for a young musician to learn in the first days is that of the lesser tone masters, together with those simpler pieces of the great composers which come within his power to comprehend—within the power of a child's hands and voice. Let us see, once again, if it is not clear:

True composers, great and small, sing from the heart. If one having a little skill turn it unworthily away from the good and true work he might do, then he does not use rightly his one talent. He does not give us true thought in tone. He writes for vanity or a low purpose, and is not a lesser master but he is untrue.

It is not our right to play anything. We may rightly play only that which is full of such good thought as we in our power may understand. It is to supply us with just this that the lesser masters write. In simple, yet clear and beautiful pictures, they tell us many and many a secret of the world of tone into which we shall some day be welcomed by the greater ones if we are faithful unto the lesser.

CHAPTER XIV.

HARMONY AND COUNTERPOINT

"Whilst I was in Florence, I did my utmost to learn the exquisite manner of Michaelangelo, and never once lost sight of it."—Benvenuto Cellini [43]

On any important music subject Schumann has something to say. So with this:

"Learn betimes the fundamental principles of harmony."
"Do not be afraid of the words theory, thorough-bass, and the like, they will meet you as friends if you will meet them so."

We now begin to feel how definitely these rules treat everything. They pick out the important subjects and tell the simplest truth about them. The meaning of these two rules is this: From the beginning we must try to understand the grammar of music. Some of the great composers could in childhood write down music with the greatest fluency. Handel, even as a boy, wrote a new church composition for every Sunday. Mozart began to write music when less than five years old, and when he was yet a boy, in Rome, he wrote down a composition,[44] sung by the choir of the Sistine Chapel, which was forbidden to the public.

Harmony and counterpoint stand to music very much as spelling and grammar stand to language. They are the fundamentals of good writing and of good—that is, of correct—thinking in music. Harmony is the art of putting tones together so as correctly to make chords. Counterpoint has to do with composing and joining together simple melodies. A modern writer[45] on counterpoint has said: "The essence of true counterpoint lies in the equal interest which should belong to ever part." By examining a few pieces of good counterpoint you will readily see just what this means. The composer has not tried to get merely a correct chord succession, such as we find in a choral. Let us play a choral; any good one of a German master will do.[46] We notice that the soprano is the principal part, and that the other voices, while somewhat melodic, tend rather to support and follow the melody than to be independent. If, now, we play a piece of counterpoint like the G-Minor Prelude by Bach,[47] we shall have quite a good piece of counterpoint, as far as separate melodies being combined is concerned. Let us play the voice-parts separately. We shall find equal melodic interest in each. The chords grow out of the music. Comparing this with the choral, the main difference between harmony and counterpoint should be clear to us. We shall observe that the three voices do not proceed in the same way. If one part moves quickly, as in the bass of the first two measures, the other parts are quieter; if the bass ceases to move rapidly some other voice will take up the motion, as we see in the third and following measures. As a general thing no two voices in contrapuntal writing move in the same way, each voice-part being contrasted with different note-values. This gives greater interest and makes each voice stand forth independently.

At first contrapuntal music may not seem interesting to us. If that is so, it is because we are not in the least degree conscious of the wonderful interest which has been put into every part. The truth is, that in the beginning we cannot fully understand the thought that has been put into the music, but by perseverance it will come to us little by little. This is what makes great music lasting. It is so deftly made, yet so delicately, that we have to go patiently in search of it. We must remember that gems have to be cut and polished from a bit of rock.

In this case the gem is the rich mind-picture which comes to us if we faithfully seek the under-thought. And the seeking is polishing the gem.

Music written entirely by the rules of counterpoint is called contrapuntal music; that written otherwise is known as free harmonic music. In the one case the composer desired to have a beautiful weaving of the parts—clear as the lines in a line-engraving. In the other, the intention is to get effects from tones united into chords, such as is obtained from masses of color in a painting. Neither form may be said to be the superior of the other. Each is valuable in its place, and each has possibilities peculiarly its own, which the other could not give. Pure counterpoint could not give us such a charming effect as Chopin obtains in the first study of Opus 10; nor could the plainer and more free harmonic style give us such delicate bits of tracery as Bach has in his fugues.

If now you will take the trouble to learn two long words, later in your study of music they will be of use to you. The first is Polyphonic; the other is Monophonic. Both, like many other words in our language, are made up of two shorter words, and come from another language—Greek. In both we have "phonic," evidently meaning the same in each case, limited or modified by the preceding part—poly and mono. Phonic is the Anglicized Greek for sound. We use it in the English word telephonic. Now if we define mono and poly we shall understand these two long words.

Mono means one, poly means many. We say _mono_tone, meaning one tone; also _poly_gon, meaning many sides.

In the musical reference monophonic music means music of one voice, rather than of one tone, and polyphonic music is that for many voices. Simple melodies with or without accompanying chords are monophonic; many melodies woven together, as in the Bach piece which we have looked over, are polyphonic.

In the history of music two men surpassed all others in what they accomplished in counterpoint—that is, in polyphonic writing. The one was Palestrina, an Italian; the other was Bach, a German. Palestrina lived at a time when the music of the church was very poor, so poor, indeed, that the clergy could no longer endure it. Palestrina, however, devoted himself earnestly to composing music strictly adapted to the church use. The parts were all melodic, and woven together with such great skill that they yet remain masterpieces of contrapuntal writing. Later Bach developed counterpoint very much more in the modern way. He did with polyphony for the piano and organ much the same as Palestrina did for the voice. There have never lived greater masters than these in the art of polyphonic music.

There is still another form of writing which is neither strictly harmonic, nor strictly contrapuntal,—it is a combination of both. There is not the plain unadorned harmonic progress as in the simple choral, nor is there the strict voice progression as in the works of Bach. This form of writing which partakes of the beauties of both the others has been called the free harmonic style. It has been followed by all the great masters since the time of Bach,[48] even before, indeed. If you can imagine a beautiful song-melody with an artistic accompaniment, so arranged that all can be played upon the piano, you will understand what the third style is. It is wonderfully free, surely; sometimes proceeding in full free chords, as in the opening measures of the B flat Sonata of Beethoven,[49] again running away from all freedom back to the old style, until the picture looks as old as a monkish costume among modern dress.

All of the great sonatas and symphonies are of this wonderfully varied form of writing. How full it can be of expressiveness you know from the Songs without Words by Mendelssohn, and the Nocturnes of Chopin; how full of flickering humor you hear in the Scherzo of a Beethoven symphony; how full of deep solemnity and grief one feels in the funeral marches.[50]

This school of composition has been followed by both the greater and the lesser masters. Every part is made to say something as naturally and interestingly as possible, being neither too restricted nor too free. Then, in playing, both hands must be equally intelligent, for each has an important part assigned to it.

The great good of study in harmony and counterpoint is that it increases one's appreciation. As soon as we begin to understand the spirit of good writing we begin to play better, because we see more. We begin, perhaps in a small way, to become real music-thinkers. By all these means we learn to understand better and better what the meaning of true writing is. It will be clear to us that a composer is one who thinks pure thoughts in tone, and not one who is a weaver of deceits.

CHAPTER XV.

MUSIC AND READING

"Truly it has been said, a loving heart is the beginning of all knowledge."—Thomas Carlyle

A beautiful thing in life is the friendship for books. Every one who loves books pays some day a tribute to them, expressing thankfulness for the joy and comfort they have given. There are in them, for everybody who will seek, wise words, good counsel, companies of great people, fairies, friends for every day, besides wonders we never see nor dream of in daily life.

Some of the great men have told us about their love for books; how they have saved penny by penny slowly to buy one, or how after the day's labor a good book and the firelight were prized above anything else. All tell us how much they owe to books and what a blessing books are.

Imagine the number of heart-thoughts there must be in a shelf full of good books! Thoughts in tones or thoughts in words may be of the heart or not. But it is only when they are of the heart that they are worthy of our time.

You will not only love books, but gain from them something of the thoughts they contain. We might, had we time, talk of classic books, but as we have already talked of classic music we know what the principal thing is. It is that good thought, out of the heart, be expressed in a scholarly way—"Great thought needs great expression."[51] This teaches us the necessity for choosing good books for our instruction and for our entertainment. They present beautiful pictures to us truthfully, or they present truth to us beautifully. And these are the first test of a written thought—its truth and its beauty.

If you read good books you will have in every volume you get something well worth owning. You should bestow upon it as much care as you would want any other good friend to receive. And if it has contributed help or pleasure to you it is surely worth an abiding place. A fine pleasure will come from a good book even after we are quite done with it. As we see it in years after it has been read there comes back to one a remembrance of all the old pleasures, and with it a sense of thankfulness for so pleasant a friendship. Hence any book that has given us joy or peace or comfort is well worth not only good care, but a place for always; as a worthy bit of property.

In the early days of your music study, it will be a pleasure to you to know that there are many and delightful books about music written, sometimes by music-lovers, sometimes by the composers. The written word-thoughts of the composers are often full of great interest. They not only reveal to us many secrets of the tone-art, but teach us much about the kinds of things and of thoughts which lived in the minds of the composers. We learn definitely not only the music-interests of the composers, but the life-interest as well. It really seems as if we were looking into their houses, seeing the way they lived and worked, and listening to their words. Never afterward do we regard the great names in music as uninteresting. The most charming and attractive pictures cluster about them and it all gives us a new inspiration to be true to music, loyal to the truth of music, and willing to do as we see others have done, and to learn by doing. The lesson we get from the life of every man is, that he must do if he would learn.

I am sure you will spend many delightful minutes with the Letters of a great composer. Every one is like a talk with the writer. They are so friendly, and so full of the heart, and yet so filled with the man himself. Especially the Letters of Mendelssohn and Schumann will please you. In truth the Letters of all the composers are among the most valuable music writings we have. In some way they seem to explain the music itself: and the composer at once becomes a close friend. But besides these read the biographies. Then it is as if we were personally invited home to the composer and shown all his ways and his life. And besides these, there are some friendly books full of the very best advice as to making us thoughtful musicians; many and many again are the writers who have so loved art—not the art of tone alone, but all other arts as well—that they have told us of it in good and earnest books which are friendly, because they are written from the right place; and that you must know by this time is the heart.

You will soon see when you have read about the composers that true music comes out of true life. Then you will begin to love true life, to be useful, and to help others. But all these things do not come at once. Yet, as we go along step by step, we learn that art is unselfish, and we must be so to enjoy it; art is truthful—we must be so to express it; art is full of life—we must know and live truth in order to appreciate it. And the study of pure thoughts in music, in books, and in our own life will help to all this.

CHAPTER XVI.

THE HANDS

"The skill of their hands still lingers."—John Ruskin [52]

In one of our Talks, speaking about the thoughts in our hearts, we said that they crept from the heart into our arms and hands, into the music we play, and off to those who hear us, causing in them the thoughts by which they judge us. Thus we see, that as Janus stands sentinel at the doorway of the year, so the hands stand between the secret world of thought within and the questioning world of curiosity without.

If we were not in such a hurry usually, we might stop to think that every one, all over the world, is training the hands for some purpose. And such a variety of purposes! One strives to get skill with tools, another is a conjurer, another spends his life among beautiful and delicate plants, another reads with his fingers.[53] In any one of these or of the countless other ways that the hands may be used, no one may truly be said to have skill until delicacy has been gained. Even in a forcible use of the hands there must be the greatest delicacy in the guidance. You can readily see that when the hands are working at the command of the heart they must be ever ready to make evident the meaning of the heart, and that is expressed in truthful delicacy. Not only are all the people in the world training their hands, but they are, as we have already said, training them in countless different ways.

Have you ever stopped to think of another matter: that all things about us, except the things that live, have been made by hands? And of the things that live very many are cared for by the hands. These thoughts will suggest something to us. Those things which are good and beautiful suggest noble use of the hands; while those which are of no service, harmful and destructive, show an ignoble use. But noble and ignoble use of the hands is only another evidence of thought. Thought that is pure in the heart guides the hands to beautiful ends. And if the heart is impure in its thoughts, of course you know what follows.

I have always been impressed in reading the books of John Ruskin to note how many times he speaks about the hands. Very truly, indeed, does he recognize that back of all hand work there is heart-thought, commanding, directing, actually building. It shows everywhere. The building of a wall with the stones rightly placed demands honor. The builder may be rude, but if his hands place the stones faithfully one upon another, there is surely honor in his heart. If it were not so his hands could not work faithfully.

If the work is finer, like that work in gold which many have learned eagerly in former times, in Rome and Florence, still the spirit must be the same. So we see, that be the work coarse or fine, it is in either case prompted by the same kind of heart-thought.

Many times in these Talks I have spoken of Ruskin's words to you; for two reasons: first, his words are always full of meaning, because he was so full of thought when he wrote them; and second, I would have you, from the first days, know something of him and elect him to your friendship. Many times he will speak to you in short, rude words, impatiently too, but never mind that, his heart is warm and full of good.

Now from what was said a moment ago about the stone work and the gold work we can understand these words:

"No distinction exists between artist and artisan, except that of higher genius or better conduct."

Learn from this then, be the work of our hands what it may, its first quality and the first things for which it shall be judged are its honor, its faithfulness, and its sincerity.

Of themselves the hands are absolutely without power. They cannot move, they cannot do good things nor bad things, they can do nothing until we command them. And how shall this be done? Surely I can understand it if you have wearied of this Talk a little. But I have said all the things just for the sake of answering this question, so that you should understand it. How do we command? not the hands alone but all we do and say?

By our THOUGHTS.

Without them there is no power whatever. Until they have commanded, the hands cannot make a motion; the feet must have direction ordered to them, the tongue must be bidden to speak, and without the command there is nothing.

Of course, all these Talks are about thoughts. But we shall need a little time to speak of them particularly. And little by little it will be clear to us all why the hands need to act thoughtfully. Now the harm of the world is done by two forces,—by evil thought and by thoughtlessness. Then it is no wonder that Ruskin speaks much about the hands, for it is thought that gives them guidance. Can you wonder, that when he says, "the idle and loud of tongue" he associates the "useless hand."[54] These things go together, and together they come either from evil thought or from lack of thought. The moment Ruskin speaks of one who uses his hands with honor, his words glow. So he speaks of the laborer, describing him as "silent, serviceable, honorable, keeping faith, untouched by change, to his country and to Heaven."

Thus, when we are earnestly asked to do something worthy with the hands every day, we can understand why. I do not mean one worthy thing, but some one particular worthy act, especially thought out by us. To do that daily with forethought will purify the heart. It will teach us to devote the hands to that which is worthy. Then another old truth that every one knows will be clear to us: "As a man—or a child, for that matter—thinketh in his heart, so he is."

Bit by bit the thoughts of this Talk will become clear to you. You will feel more friendly toward them. Then you will really begin to think about hands; your own hands and everybody's hands. You will become truthful of hand, guiding your own thoughtfully; watching those of others carefully. And you will find that in the smallest tasks of your hands you can put forethought, while every use to which people put their hands will teach you something if you observe carefully. It may be folding a paper or picking up a pin, or anything else quite common; that matters not, common things, like any others, can be done rightly.

By this observation we shall see hands performing all sorts of odd tricks. The fingers are drumming, twitching, twirling, closing, opening, doing a multitude of motions which mean what? Nothing, do you say? Oh! no, indeed; not nothing but something. Fingers and hands which perform all these unnecessary motions are not being commanded by the thoughts, and are acting as a result of no thought; that is, of thoughtlessness. Every one does it do you say? No, that is not true. Many do these things, but those who command their thoughts never allow it. If we never moved the hands except in a task when we commanded them, we should soon become hand-skilled. The useless movements I have spoken of _un_skill the hand. They are undoing motions, and teach us that we must govern ourselves if we would become anything. Do you know how it is that people do great things? They command themselves. Having determined to do something, they work and work and work to finish it at any cost. That gives strength and character.

Having observed the hands and their duties, we can readily see the kind of task they must do in music. It is just the same kind of task as laying a wall of stone. Every motion must be done honorably. Everything must be thought out in the mind and heart before the hands are called upon to act. Wise people always go about their tasks this way. Unwise people try the other way, of acting first and thinking it out afterward, and, of course, they always fail. You can now understand that a great pianist is one who has great thought with which to command the hands. And to be sure they will obey his commands at once, he has made them obey him continuously for years. This teaching the hands to obey is called Practice.

The Italian artist, Giotto, once said:

"You may judge my masterhood of craft by seeing that I can draw a circle unerringly."

CHAPTER XVII.

WHAT THE ROMAN LADY SAID

"You may always be successful if you do but set out well, and let good thoughts and practice proceed upon right method."—Marcus Aurelius [55]

The same wise Roman emperor who said this tells us a very pretty thing about his mother, which shows us what a wise lady she must have been, and how in the days of his manhood, with the cares of a great nation upon him, he yet pondered upon the childhood teaching of home. First, he speaks of his grandfather Verus, who, by his example, taught him not to be prone to anger; then of his father, the

Emperor Antoninus Pius, from whom he learned to be modest and manly; then of his mother, whose name was Domitia Calvilla. Let us read some of his own words about her, dwelling particularly upon a few of them. He writes: "As for my mother, she taught me to have regard for religion, to be generous and open-handed, and not only to forbear from doing anybody an ill turn, but not so much as to endure the thought of it."

Now these words are the more wonderful when we remember that they were not taken down by a scribe in the pleasant apartments of the royal palace in Rome, but were written by the Emperor himself on the battlefield; for this part of his famous book is signed: "Written in the country of the Quadi."

In our last Talk on the Hands we came to the conclusion, that unless the hands were commanded they could not act. And on inquiring as to what gave these commands we found it was the thoughts. Many people believe it is perfectly safe to think anything, to have even evil thoughts in their hearts, for thoughts being hidden, they say, cannot be seen by others. But a strange thing about thought is this: The moment we have a thought, good or bad, it strives to get out of us and become an action. And it most always succeeds. Not at once, perhaps, for thoughts like seeds will often slumber a long time before they spring into life. So it becomes very clear to us that if we wish to be on the alert we must not watch our actions, but look within and guard the thoughts; for they are the springs of action.

You now see, I am sure, how wise the Emperor's mother was in teaching her boy not even to endure a thought to do evil unto others. For the thought would get stronger and stronger, and suddenly become an action. Certainly; and hence the first thing to learn in this Talk is just these words:

Thoughts become actions.

That is an important thing. In a short time you will see, that if you do not learn it you can never enjoy music, nor beautiful things, nor the days themselves. Let us see how this will come about.

I have told your teacher[56] the name of the book which was written by the Roman lady's boy. Well, in that book, running through it like a golden thread, is this bit of teaching from his mother.

Not only did he think of it and write it on the battlefield, but at all times there seemed to come to him more and more wisdom from it. And he tells us this same thought over and over again in different words. Sometimes it leads him to say very droll things; for instance:

"Have you any sense in your head? Yes. Why do you not make use of it then? For if this does its part, for what more can you wish?"[57] Then, a very good thought which we frequently hear:

"Your manners will very much depend upon what you frequently think."[58] There are many others, but these show us that the meaning of his mother's words went deep, teaching that not action must be guarded but the thought which gives rise to action. Now, what can be the value of speaking about the Roman lady? Let us see.

In music, the tones are made either by the hands or by the voice. And to make a tone is to do something. This doing something is an action, and action comes from thought. No music, then, can be made unless it be made by thinking. And the right playing of good music must come from the right thinking of good thoughts. It may be that you will hear some one say that to think good thoughts is not needed in making good music. Never believe it! Bad thought never made anything good, and never will because it never can. In the very first days you must learn, that good things of all kinds come from good thoughts, because they can come from nothing else.

Here, then, is the second truth of this Talk:

Good music being the fruit of good thought can be played rightly only by one who thinks good thoughts.

This leads us to another matter. First, let us see if everything is clear. True music is written out of good thought; hence, when we begin to study music we are really becoming pupils of good thought. We are learning the thoughts good men have had, trying to feel their truth and meaning, and from them learning to have our own thoughts not only good but constantly better and better. This now seems simple and necessary. We see that if we would faithfully study a composer's work it must be our principal aim to get into his heart. Then everything will be clear to us.

But we can never find our way to the heart of another until we have first found our way somewhere else. Where, do you think? To our own hearts, being willing to be severe with ourselves; not to be deceitful in our own eyes; not to guard the outer act, but the inner thought; not to study nor to be what seems, but what is.[59] This may seem a long and roundabout way of learning to play music, but it is the honest, straightforward way of going to the great masters whom we wish to know.

In one of the books of the Greek general, Xenophon,[60] Socrates is made to say that men do nothing without fire; and quite in the same way we may learn nothing of each other, especially of those greater than ourselves, without thought; which should be pure, strong, inquiring, and kind. With this we may do all.

Thus far we have two principles. Let us review them:

I. Thoughts become actions.

II. Good music being the fruit of good thought can be played rightly only by one who thinks good thoughts.

Now, is it not clear that this can come about only when we watch over our own thoughts and govern them as if they were the thoughts of others? And when we do not so much as endure the thought of harm or evil or wrong we shall be living in the spirit of the Roman lady whose son's life was lived as his mother taught.

CHAPTER XVIII.

THE GLORY OF THE DAY

"Be not anxious about to-morrow. Do to-day's duty, fight today's temptation; and do not weaken and disturb yourself by looking forward to things which you cannot see, and could not understand if you saw them."—Charles Kingsley

Nearly all of us have heard about the little child who one day planted seeds and kept constantly digging them up afterward to see if they were growing. No doubt the child learned that a seed needs not only ground and care, but time. When it is put in the earth it begins to feel its place and to get at home; then, if all is quite right,—but not otherwise—it sends out a tiny rootlet as if it would say that it trusts and believes the earth will feed that rootlet. And if the earth is kind the root grows and finds a solid foothold. At the same time there is another thing happening. When the seed finds it can trust itself to root it feels no longer afraid to show itself. It goes down, down quietly for a firmer hold, and upward feeling the desire for light.

A firm hold and more light, we cannot think too much of what they mean.

Every day that the seed pushes its tender leaves and stem upward it has more and more to encounter. The rains beat it down; the winds bend it to the very earth from which it came; leaves and weeds bury it beneath their strength and abundance, but despite all these things, in the face of death itself, the brave little plant strongly keeps its place. It grows in the face of danger. But how? Day after day, as it fights its way in the air and sunshine, blest or bruised as it may be, the little plant never fails to keep at one thing. That is, to get a firmer and firmer hold. From that it never lets go. Break its leaves and its stem, crush it as you will, stop its upward growth even, but as long as there is a spark of life in it there will be more roots made. It aims from the first moment of its life to get hold strongly.

And it seems as if the plant has always a great motive. The moment it feels it has grasped the mother-earth securely with its roots it turns its strength to making something beautiful. In the air and light, in the dark earth even, every part of the plant is seeking for the means to do a wonderful thing. It drinks in the sunshine, and with the warmth of it, and to the glory of its own life, it blossoms. It has come from a tiny helpless seed to a living plantlet with the smallest stem and root, and while the stem fights for a place in the air the root never ceases to get a strong hold of the dear earth in which the plant finds its home. Then when the home is firmly secured and the days have made the plant stronger and more shapely, it forgets all the rude winds and rain and the drifting leaves, and shows how joyful it is to live by giving something.

Then it is clear that every hardship had its purpose. The rains beat it down, but at the same time they were feeding it; the leaves dropped about and covered it, but that protected its tenderness: and thus in all the trials it finds a blessing. Its growth is stronger, and thankful for all its life it seeks to express this thankfulness. In its heart there is something it is sure. And true enough, out it comes some day in a flower with its color and tenderness and perfume; all from the earth, but taken from it by love which the plant feels for the ground as its home.

We can see from this, that the beauty of a plant or of a tree is a sign of its relation to the earth in which it lives. If its hold is weak—if it loosely finds a place for a weak root—it lies on the ground, helpless, strengthless, joyless. But firmly placed and feeling safe in its security, it gives freely of its blossoms; or, year after year, like a tree, shows us its wonderous mass of leaf, all of it a sign that earth and tree are truely united.

It has been said, and no doubt it is true, that one who cares for plants and loves them becomes patient. The plant does not hurry; its growth is slow and often does not show itself; and one who cares for them learns their way of being and of doing. The whole lesson is that of allowing time, and by using it wisely to save it. The true glory of a day for a plant is the air and sunlight and earth-food which it has taken, from which it has become stronger. And every day, one by one, as it proves, contributes something to its strength.

All men who have been patient students of the earth's ways have learned to be careful, to love nature, and to take time. And we all must learn to take time. It is not by careless use that we gain anything, but by putting heart and mind into what must be done. When heart and mind enter our work they affect time curiously; because of the great interest we take in what we do time is not thought of; and what is not thought of, is not noticed.

Hence, the value of time comes to this: to use any time we may have, much or little, with the heart in the task. When that is done there is not only better work accomplished but there are no regrets lingering about to make us feel uncomfortable.

A practice hour can only be an hour of unwelcome labor when one thinks so of it. If we go to the piano with interest in the playing we shall be unconscious of time. Many men who love their labor tell of sitting for hours at their work not knowing that hours have gone by.

If there is a love for music in any of us it will grow as a seed. And as the seed needs the dear mother-earth, so the music needs the heart. When it has taken root there and becomes firmer and firmer it will begin to show itself outwardly as the light of the face. After it is strong and can bear up against what assails it—not the wind and the rain and the dry leaves, but discouragement and hard correction and painful hot tears—then with that strength it will flourish.

Now, sometimes, in the days of its strength the music will seek far more in its life, just as the plant seeks for more and blossoms. The flower in the music is as great for all as for one. It is joy and helpfulness. When for the love of music one seeks to do good then music has borne its blossom.

Thus, by learning the life of a simple plant we learn the true mission of the beautiful art of tone. It must put forth deeply its roots into the heart that it may be fed. It must strive for strength as it grows against whatever may befall it. It must use its food of the heart and its strength for a pure purpose, and there is but one—to give joy.

This turns our thoughts to two things: First, to the men and women who by their usefulness and labor increased the meaning of music. This is the glory of their days. Second, we look to ourselves with feeble hands and perhaps little talent, and the thought comes to us, that with all we have we are to seek not our own glorification but the joy of others.

CHAPTER XIX.

THE IDEAL

"Le beau est aussi utile que l'utile, plus peutêtre."—Victor Hugo

Mozart once had a friend named Gottfried von Jacquin, who was a man of careful thought, and evidently a good musician,—for we are told that a melody composed by him is frequently said, even to this day, to be by Mozart. This Gottfried lived in Vienna with his father, and to their house Mozart often went. At this time Mozart had an album in which his friends were invited to write. Among the verses is a sentiment written by Gottfried von Jacquin, saying:

"True genius is impossible without heart; no amount of intellect alone or of imagination, no, nor of both together, can make genius. Love is the soul of genius."

Here we have the same truth told us which we have already found for ourselves, namely, that all good music comes from the heart. We have found it by studying music and striving faithfully to get deep into its real meaning. But today we have the words of one who was enabled to watch closely as a friend one of the greatest composers that ever lived. And being much with him, hearing the music of the master played by the master himself, put the thought into his head, that it is impossible to be a true genius without heart and love.

From this we shall have courage to know that what we pursue in music is real; that the beauties of great music, though they may just now be beyond us, are true, and exist to those who are prepared for them. When in our struggle to be more capable in art than we are to-day we think of the beauty around us, and desire to be worthy of it, we are then forming an ideal, and ideals are only of value when we strive to live up to them.

Once in Rome there lived a Greek slave—some day you may read his name. He has told us, that "if thou wouldst have aught of good, have it from thyself."[61] Of course we see in this, immediately, the truth that has been spoken of in nearly every one of these Talks. It is this: We must, day by day, become better acquainted with ourselves, study our thoughts, have purity of heart, and work for something.

Now, working for something may be accomplished in a simple manner without thinking of it. If every task is done in our best way it adds something to us. It is true and beautiful, too, that the reward for patient, faithful work comes silently to us, and often we do not know of its presence. But some day, finding ourselves stronger, we look to know the cause of it, and we see that the faithfulness of past days has aided us.

So art teaches us a very practical lesson in the beginning. If we would have her favors we must do her labors. If we say to music: "I should love to know you;" music says to us,

"Very well, work and your wish shall be gratified." But without that labor we cannot have that wish. The Greek slave knew that and said:

"Thou art unjust, if thou desire to gain those things for nothing."

Now we begin to see that art has no gifts to bestow upon us for nothing. Many think it has, and pursue it until the truth dawns upon them; then, because of their error, they dislike it. To recognize the truth about art and to pursue that truth, despite the hard road, is to have courage. And the Ideal is nothing else than the constant presence of this truth.

And what do we gain by pursuing it? Not common pleasure, but true happiness; not uncertainty, but true understanding; not selfish life, but true and full life. And we can see the beauty of art in nothing more plainly than in the fact that all these things may come to a child, and a new and brighter life is made possible by them.

The very first day we came together, the little child said to the master:

"Master, I do not understand what thou hast said, yet I believe thee."

It is hard, sometimes, to feel the truth and to keep it with us; hard, not only for a child, but for any one; and yet, if with faith we will labor with it until the light comes, then we are truly rewarded and made richer according to our faith.

We must not forget in the first days, as we leave our music, that the path we have taken since we came together is the hardest; not for always, but for now. The right path is hard at first—the wrong one is hard always.

We will understand it all better in other days if we remain faithful now. If, however, we should forget for a moment that art demands our loyalty, there will be no joy or peace in it for us. Worse, perhaps, than starting out upon the wrong path, is the deserting of the right one. Sometimes out of impatience we do this; out of impatience and self-love, which is the worst of all. "Truth is the beginning of all good, and the greatest of all evils is self-love."[62]

With the trials that music costs us, with its pains and discouragements, we might easily doubt all these promises which are contained in our ideals, but we shall be forever saved from deserting them if we remember that these ideals have been persistently held by great men. They have never given them up. One of the strongest characteristics of Bach and of Beethoven was their determination to honor their thoughts. Sometimes we find the same persistence and faithfulness in lesser men.

I am sure you will see this faith beautifully lived in the few facts we have about the life of Johann Christian Kittel, a pupil of Bach, and it is strongly brought out by the pretty story told of him, that when pleased with a pupil's work he would draw aside a curtain which covered a portrait of Bach and let the faithful one gaze upon it for a moment. That was to him the greatest reward he could give for faithfulness in the music task.

And this reminds us of how the teacher, Pistocchi, who, in teaching the voice, kept in mind a pure tone, a quiet manner of singing, and the true artistic way of doing. Among his pupils was a certain Antonio Bernacchi, who, after leaving his master, began to display his voice by runs and trills and meaningless tones. And this he did, not because of true art, for that was not it, but because it brought him the applause of unthinking people.

Once, when the master, Pistocchi, heard him do this he is said to have exclaimed: "Ah, I taught thee how to sing, and now thou wilt play;" meaning that the true song was gone and the pupil no longer sang out of the heart, but merely out of the throat. Pistocchi kept his ideal pure.

We have then among our ideals two of first importance. The ideal perception of music, as being the true heart-expression of great men; and the ideal of our doings, which is the true heart-expression of ourselves. And to keep these ideals is difficult in two ways: The difficulty of keeping the pure intention of great men ever before us, and the difficulty of keeping close and faithful to the tasks assigned us. Then we can say with the little child:

"Master, I do not understand what thou hast said, yet I believe thee."

CHAPTER XX.

THE ONE TALENT

"Then he which had received the one talent came."—Matthew, XXV: 24

Some day, when you read about the great composers, you will be delighted with the pictures of their home-life. You will see how they employed music every day. In all cases, as we study them, we learn how very much they have sacrificed for the music they love, studying it daily because of the joy which it yields them. We see them as little children, eager to be taught, wanting to listen to music, and to hear about it. Many of the composers whose child-life is thus interesting were children in very poor families, where things were neither fine nor beautiful, where the necessary things of life were not plentiful, and where all had to be careful and saving so that every bit should be made to go as far as possible. The eagerness and determination of some children in music-history is really wonderful. It is the true determination. And you are not surprised, in following it, to note that it leads the children who have it into lives of great usefulness.

All through the life of Handel we find determination running like a golden thread. He was just as determined to be a musician as Lincoln was to get an education when he read books by the firelight. Handel's father was a surgeon, and knew so little about music that he failed entirely to understand the child. He not only forbade the boy to study music, but even kept him away from school that he might not by any chance learn to read the notes. But one who was in future years to befriend homeless children and to write wondrous music for all the world could not be held back by such devices. By some means, and with friendly assistance (perhaps his mother's), he succeeded in smuggling into the garret a spinet, which is a kind of piano. By placing cloth upon the strings he so deadened the wires that no one downstairs could hear the tones when the spinet was played. And day after day this little lad would sit alone in his garret, learning more and more about the wonders which his heart and his head told him were in the tiny half-dumb spinet before him. Not the more cheerful rooms down-stairs nor the games of his playmates drew him away from the music he loved, the music which he felt in his heart, remember.

One would expect such determination to show itself in many ways. It did. Handel does not disappoint us in this. All through his life he had strong purposes and a strong will—concentration—which led him forward. You know how he followed his father's coach once. Perhaps it was disobedience,—but what a fine thing happened when he reached the duke's palace and played the organ. From that day every one knew that his life would be devoted to music. Sometimes at home, sometimes in foreign lands, he was always working, thinking, learning. He is said, in his boyhood, to have copied large quantities of music, and to have composed something every week. This copying made him better acquainted with other music, and the early habit of composition made it easy for him to write his thoughts in after years. Indeed, so skilled did he become, that he wrote one opera—"Rinaldo"—in fourteen days, and the "Messiah" was written in twenty-four days.[63]

Yet parts of his great works he wrote and rewrote until they were exactly as they should be. It will do is a thought that never comes into the head of a great artist. How do you imagine such a man was to his friends? We are told that, "he was in character at once great and simple." And again it has been said that, "his smile was like heaven."

We have seen Handel as the great composer, but he was not so busy in this that his thoughts were not also dwelling upon other things. If ever you go to London, you should of a Sunday morning hear the service at the Foundling Hospital. You will see there many hundreds of boys and girls grouped about the organ. Their singing will seem beautiful to you, from its sweetness and from the simple faith in which it is done. After the service you may go to the many rooms of this home for so many otherwise homeless ones.

There are for you to visit: the playroom, the schoolroom, the long halls with the pretty white cots, and the pleasant dining-room. Here it will please you to see the little ones march into dinner, with their similar dresses, and all looking as happy as possible. But the picture you will, no doubt, longest keep, is that of the children about the organ.

They will tell you there that it was Handel who gave this organ to the chapel, and who, for the benefit of the children who might come here, gave concerts, playing and conducting, which were so successful that they had to be repeated. A "fair copy" of the "Messiah" will be shown you as one of the precious possessions.

It will very plainly be present in your mind how the little boy sat alone playing day after day in the garret, wishing no better pastime than to express the feelings of his heart in tones. Perhaps you will think of his words: "Learn (of) all there is to learn, then choose your own path." He will appeal to you as having possessed an "early completeness of character," which abided always with him. It is evident in following the life of Handel, and it would be equally plain with any other composer, that great talent is developed out of a small beginning, and if small, is yet earnest and determined. From the first days of a great man's life to the last we find constant effort. "I consider those live best who study best to become as good as possible."[64] Music helps us to keep the upper windows open; that is why it does so much for us even if we have but one talent.

To develop our one talent is a duty, just as it is a duty to develop two or five talents. It is given to us to increase. And no one knows how much joy may come to us and to others from the growing of that talent. We gain much in power to give pleasure to others, if the talent we have be made stronger by faithful effort. As we have seen good come forth from the story of the man with many talents, we can see how, similarly, he with one talent has also great power with which he may add unto himself and others.

In all of our Talks it has been evident from what we have said, that music is a beautiful art to us, even though we may have but little of it. But equally we have learned, that for ever so little we must prove ourselves worthy. We must honestly give something for all we get. This is the law, and the purpose of all our Talks is to learn it.

We have, likewise, learned that true music, out of the heart, may not at the first please us, but within it there is a great deal and we must seek it. The history of all who have faithfully studied the works of the great masters is, that for all the thought and time one spends in studying master works a great gain comes. On the other hand, everybody's experience with common music is, that while it may please much at first and even captivate us, yet it soon tires us so that we can scarcely listen patiently to it.

Still a further lesson is, that working with many talents or with one is the same. Talents, one or many, are for increase and faithful development. Handel's life was a determined struggle to make the most of his power. It should be ours.

CHAPTER XXI.

LOVE FOR THE BEAUTIFUL

"Every color, every variety of form, has some purpose and explanation."—Sir John Lubbock [65]

Now, when we are almost at the end of the way we have traveled together, it will be natural to look back upon the road over which we have come. Not all of it will be visible, to be sure. We have forgotten this pleasant scene and that; others, however, remain fresh in our minds. And as the days pass and we think over our way there will now and again come to us a scene, a remembrance, so full of beauty and of pleasure that we shall feel rich in the possession of it.

To me there is nothing we have learned together greater in value, richer in truth and comfort than the thought that the beautiful in music and in art is at the same time the good. Even if a person is not at all times good, there is raised in him the feeling of it whenever he consciously looks upon a beautiful object. We see in this how wise it is for one to choose to have beautiful things, to surround others with them, to love them, and to place reverent hands upon them.

We can never make a mistake about gentle hands. Once a lady said to a boy:

"You should touch all things with the same delicacy that one should bestow upon a tender flower. It shows that deep within yourself you are at rest, that you make your hands go forward to a task carefully and with much thought. In the roughest games you play do not forget this; then your hands shall be filled with all the thought you have within yourself."

Sometimes, when I am in a great gallery, the thought is very strong in me, that many (ever, and ever so many) people, in all countries and in all times, have so loved the beautiful as to devote their lives to it. Painters, who have made pictures to delight men for generations, looked and looked and prayed to find the beautiful. And we must believe that one looks out of the heart to find the beautiful or he finds only the common. And the sculptors who have loved marble for the delight they have in beautiful forms, they, too, with eyes seeking beauty, and hands so gentle upon the marble that it almost breathes for them, they, too, have loved the beautiful.

But commoner ones have the tenderest love for what is sweet and fair in life,—people who are neither painters nor sculptors. In their little way—but it is a true way—they have sunlight in their hearts, and with it love for something.

Perhaps it is a flower. I have been told of a man—in fact I have seen him—who could do the cruelest things; who was so bad that he could not be permitted to go free among others, and yet he loved plants so much that if they were put near him he would move quietly among them, touching this one and that; gazing at them, and acting as if he were in another world. As we said once before about the spring, so we may say here about love for the beautiful: it may be covered up with every thing that is able to keep it down, but it is always there.

It is always pleasanter to hear about people and their ways than to heed advice. But people and their ways often set us good examples; and we were curious, indeed, if we did not look sharply at ourselves to see just what we are. From all we have been told about the beautiful we can at least learn this: that it sweetens life; that it makes even a common life bright; that if we have it in us it may be as golden sunlight to some poor one who is in the darkness of ignorance, that is the advantage and the beauty of all good things in our lives, namely, the good it may be unto others. And the beautiful music we may sing or play is not to show what we are or what we can do—it will, of course do these things— but it is to be a blessing to those who listen. And how are blessings bestowed? Out of the heart.

Once there was a nobleman[66] with power and riches. He loved everything. Learning and art and all had he partaken of. But the times were troubled in his country, and for some reason he lost all he had and was imprisoned. Then there was scarcely anything in his life. All he had was the cell, the prison-yard, and, now and again, a word or two with his keeper. The cell was small and gloomy, the keeper silent, the yard confined and so closely paved with cobblestones that one could scarcely see the earth between them.

Yes, indeed, it was a small world and a barren one into which they had forced him. But he had his thoughts, and daily as he walked in his confined yard, they were busy with the past, weaving, weaving. What patterns they made, and he, poor one, was sometimes afraid of them! But still they kept on weaving, weaving.

One day, as he walked in his yard, he noticed that between two of the stones there seemed to be something and he looked at it. With the greatest attention he studied it, then he knelt on the rude stones and looked and looked again. His heart beat and his hands trembled, but yet with a touch as gentle as any one could give, he moved a grain or two of soil and there, beneath, was something which the poor captive cried out for joy to see—a tiny plant. As if in a new world, and certainly as if another man, he cared daily for the tender little companion that had come to share his loneliness; he thought of it first in the morning and last at night. He gave it of his supply of water and, as a father, he watched over it.

And it grew so that one day he saw that his plant must either die or have more room. And it could not have more room unless a cobblestone were removed. Now this could only be done with the consent of the Emperor. Well, let us not stop to hear about the way he found, but he did get his request to the Emperor and, after a while, what happened do you think? That the plant was given more room? Yes, that is partly it, and the rest is this: the prisoner himself was given more room—he was liberated.

Just because the seed of a beautiful thing came to life in his tiny world he found love for it and a new life, a care, something outside of himself. And it brought him all.

That love which is not given to self reveals the beauty of the world.

CHAPTER XXII.

IN SCHOOL

"Every successive generation becomes a living memorial of our public schools, and a living example of their excellence."—Joseph Story

In these days we learn many things in our schools—even music. They surely must have a purpose, all the studies and the music as well. Let us in this Talk see if we can find what the purpose is.

It costs our Government a great deal to educate the children of the land. There are now nearly twenty million children in our country. That is a number you cannot conceive. But every morning of the year, when it is not a vacation day, you may think of this vast number leaving home and going to school to be taught. I am sure the picture will make us all think how wise a Government is that devotes so much to making us know more, because by learning more we are able to enjoy more, to do more, to be more. And this makes us better citizens.

Year after year, as men study and learn about what is best to have children taught in school, the clearer it becomes that what is given is dictated because of its usefulness. Arithmetic teaches us to calculate our daily affairs. Grammar teaches us to listen and to speak understandingly. Penmanship and Spelling teach us properly to make the signs which represent speech. Geography teaches us of the earth on which we live, and how we may travel about it. History teaches us how to understand the doings of our own day and makes us acquainted with great men of former times, who by striving have earned a place in our remembrance.

As we go on in our school education, taking up new studies, we find to a still greater degree that what we learn is for usefulness. Arithmetic becomes mathematics in general. Grammar is brought before us in other languages, and branches out into the study of Rhetoric and Literature. History is taught us of many lands, particularly of Greece, Rome, and England. And, bit by bit, these various histories merge into one, until, perhaps not until college years or later, the doings of the countries in all the centuries of which we have knowledge is one unbroken story to us. We know the names of lands and of people. Why Greece could love art, why Rome could have conquest; why these countries and all their glories passed away to give place to others; all these things become clear to us. We learn of generals, statesmen, poets, musicians, rulers. Their characters are made clear; their lives are given to us in biography, and year after year the story of the earth and man is more complete, more fascinating, more helpful to us in learning our own day.

Then, besides all these studies, we are taught to do things with the hands. After the Talks we have already had about doing, we know what it means to have training of the hands. It really means the training of the thoughts. We are training the mind to make the hands perform their tasks rightly. It is the same in the science lesson which teaches us to see; actually to use our eyes until we see things. That may not seem to be a difficult task, but there are really very few people who can accurately and properly use their eyes. If there were more, fewer mistakes would be made.

Thus we can see that school work divides its tasks into two general classes:

First, the learning of facts.

Second, the actual doing of things.

You will readily see that to do things properly is possible only when we know facts which tell us how to do them. That shows you at once the wisdom of the education you receive.

Now, let us imagine that school life is over. For many years you have gone faithfully every day to your place, you have done your tasks as honestly as you could, and said your lessons, being wounded no doubt by failures, but gladdened again by successes. Now, when it is all over, what is there of it?

Well, above all things, there is one truth of it which it is wonderful people do not think of more frequently. And that truth is this: The only education we may use in our own life is that which we have ourselves. No longer have we help of companions or teachers. We depend entirely upon our own personal knowledge. If we speak it is our own knowledge of Grammar that is used. We cannot have a book at hand in order to know from it the words we should use. If we make a calculation about money, or do anything with numbers, it must be done from our knowledge of Arithmetic, and it must be right or people will very soon cease to deal with us. Then, if we have a letter from a friend, we must of ourselves know how to read it, and if we have aught to say to another at a distance, we must be able clearly to express ourselves in writing, so that we may make no mistake in our meaning.

And this, likewise, is to be said of all the rest. Our knowledge of History, of Geography, of men of past times, of the boundaries of countries, of cities, of people, of everything, must come from ourselves. And, further yet, according as we have been careful to see in the right way and to do in the right way while we were under instruction in school, so we shall be likely to see and to do when we are not in school, and no longer have some one over us who will kindly and patiently correct our errors, teach us new ways, and give us greater powers. We may, of course, go on learning after our school days are ended; and really much of the best education comes then, if we will immediately set about correcting the faults which we find in ourselves.

Indeed, many men have gained the best part of their education after leaving school, where, perhaps, it was their fortune to stay but a short time.[67] But we must remember that the habits of learning, doing, seeking, are gained in early years, and if they are not gained then they rarely come.

Now, what have we learned about schools and school-tasks? We have learned a little of the purpose which lies in the education we receive; that out of it must come the power to do and to know; that is our own power; not that of any one else. We have seen the usefulness of school-studies, and how practical they are in our daily life.

In all this Talk we have said nothing about Music. If, however, we understand what the other studies mean, what their purpose is, we shall learn something which shall be valuable when we come to study the meaning and purpose of music in schools. That shall be our next Talk.

CHAPTER XXIII.

MUSIC IN SCHOOL

"Become in early years well-informed concerning the extent of the four voices.

"Try, even with a poor voice, to sing at sight without the aid of an instrument; from that your ear will constantly improve. In case, however, that you have a good voice, do not hesitate a moment to cultivate it; and believe, at the same time, that heaven has granted you a valuable gift."—Robert Schumann [68]

In the previous Talk we learned two very important facts about school studies. They were these:

I. They are useful.

II. They are useful in proportion to our own (not to anybody else's) real knowledge of them.

We do not study useless subjects, and it is not from our books, nor from our teacher that we go through life, making our way. In other words, the harder we work, the more independent we become; and the more independent we become, the more power we have to help others.

Now, whatever is true about other school studies is likewise true about music. It is given to children in school because it is useful, and because a child can gain power by learning it. Let us see about this.

To one who does not think deeply, it might seem that if any study in school is merely ornamental, that study is music. He might say that all the other studies tend to some practical end in life and business: that one could not add, nor read, nor transact business, nor write a letter any more correctly by knowing music. It is only an unthinking person—none other—who would say that.

Of the usefulness of all the school studies we have spoken. We need only to take a few steps along the pleasant road, about which we have had so many Talks, and we shall see how much music means in life. To us it is already plain. Music is a new world, to enter which cultivates new senses, teaches us to love the beautiful, and makes us watchful of two of the most important things in life: the thoughts and the heart. We must have exact thoughts or the music is not made aright, and the heart may be what it will, music tells all about it. Therefore, let it be good.

But music in school brings us to daily tasks in tone. What do we learn? After the difficulties of reading the notes and making the voice responsive are somewhat overcome, we study for greater power in both, the one-, two-, or three-part exercises and songs; the exercises for skill and the songs to apply the skill, and make us acquainted with the music of great masters.

In one Talk, one of the first, we spoke of the major scale. It has eight tones only, and though it has existed for many hundreds of years, no one has yet dreamed of all the wonderful tone-pictures which are contained in it. It is out of it that all the great composers have written their works, and for centuries to come men will find in it beauties great, and pure, and lasting.

As we sing in school, we are learning to put the major scale to some use. It calls upon us in the melodies which it expresses, to be careful that each tone shall be right in length, in pitch, in loudness, in place. We must sing exactly with the others, not offensively loud, nor so softly as to be of no service. And this demands precision of us; and precision demands thought. And if we are singing to gain a better use of voice we must, in every sound we make, have our thoughts exactly upon what we are doing. This is Concentration. If, on the other hand, we are trying our skill on a song, we shall have, in addition, to be careful to give the right expression, to sing not only the tones clearly, but the words, to feel the true sentiment both of the poem and of the music, and to express from our hearts as much of the meaning of poet and composer as we understand. All these things are more particularly required of us if we are singing in parts. The melody must be properly sustained and must not cover the under parts; while the under parts themselves should never intrude upon the melody, nor fail to be a good background for it. The singing of part music is one of the best ways to train the attention—that is, to get Concentration. As we sing our part we must have in mind these things:

I. To keep to it and not be drawn away by another part.

II. To give the part we sing its due prominence.

III. Never to destroy the perfect equality of the parts by unduly hastening or holding back.

IV. To remember that each part is important. The other singers have as much to think of and to do as we have, and they are entitled to just as much praise.

V. To be alert to take up our part at exactly the right place.

VI. To put the full meaning of the poet and of the composer into every word and tone.

These, after all, are only a few of the things; but from them we may learn this, that to sing (and to play is quite the same) is one of the most delicate tasks we can learn to perform, requiring attention from us in many ways at the same time. Even now the usefulness of music is clear, for the faculties we learn to employ in music form a power that can be applied in anything.

But music has even a greater reward for us than this. It presents to us many kinds of thoughts and pictures,—of bravery, of thoughtfulness, of gaiety, and others without number—and then it demands that we shall study so as to sing them truthfully from our hearts. And when we can do this music is then a joy to us and to others.

Now we see that music, just like the other studies, is useful and gives us the power to do something. And besides its use and power it is, perhaps more than any other study, the greatest means of giving happiness to others. But of that there is yet a word to be said. That shall be our next Talk.

CHAPTER XXIV.

HOW ONE THING HELPS ANOTHER

"Music washes away from the soul the dust of everyday life."—Berthold Auerbach

Just at the end of our Talk about Music in School, I said that music was the most powerful of all the studies for giving joy to others. In this Talk we shall try to learn what the studies do for each other.

Once more—and we must never get tired if the same thought comes again and again—let us remember that music is thought expressed in tone. Classic music is great and strong thought; poor, unworthy music is weak, perhaps wrong or mean thought.

Further, we have learned that thought may be good and pure, and yet that of itself is not sufficient. It must be well expressed. In short, to thought of the right sort we must add knowledge, so that it may be set before others in the right way.

Now, it is true that the more knowledge we have, the more we can do with music. We can put more meaning into it; we can better perform all the exacting duties it demands; we can draw more meaning from its art, and we can see more clearly how great a genius the composer is. Besides these things, a well-trained mind gets more thoughts from a subject than an untrained mind. Some day you will see this more clearly by observing how much better you will be able to understand your own language by possessing a knowledge of Greek and Latin.

All the school studies have a use, to be sure—a direct use—in giving us something to help us in life in one way and another. But besides this, we get another help from study; namely, the employment of the mind in the right way. For the right way of doing things which are worthy of the heart, gives power and good. It is the wrong way of doing things that causes us trouble. Some studies demand exactness above all this,—like the study of Arithmetic—others a good memory,—like History—others tax many faculties, as we have seen in our Talk about School Music.

Some of the studies are particularly valuable to us at once because they make us do. They may be called doing studies. In Arithmetic there is a result, and only one result, to be sought. In Grammar every rule we learn is to be applied in our speech. Manual training demands judgment and the careful use of the hands. Penmanship is a test for the hand, but History is a study touching the memory more than the doing faculty.

School music, you see at once, is a doing study. Not only that, it is full of life, attractive, appealing to the thoughts in many ways, and yet it is a hearty study—by that I mean a study for the heart.

If you have noticed in your piano music the Italian words which are given at the beginning of compositions, you may have thought how expressive most of them are of the heart and of action. They are doing words particularly. Allegro is cheerful; that is its true meaning. It directs us to make the music sound cheerful as we sing it or play it. What for? So that the cheerfulness of the composer shall be for us and for other people. And Vivace is not merely quickly, but vivaciously. Now what does vivacious mean? It means what its root-word vivere means, to live. It is a direction that the music must be full of life; and the true life of happiness and freedom from care is meant. So with Modcrato, a doing word which tells us very particularly how to do; namely, not too fast, spoiling it by haste, nor too slowly, so that it seems to drag, but in a particular way, that is, with moderation.

Music takes its place as a doing study; and as we have already discovered, its doing is of many kinds, all requiring care. Singing or playing is doing; reading the notes is doing; studying out the composer's meaning is doing; making others feel it is doing; everything is doing; and doing is true living, provided it is unselfish.

Let us see if there is not a simple lesson in all this. To seek it we shall have to say old thoughts over again. Music itself uses the same tones over and over again; it is by doing so that we begin to understand tone a little.

The school studies try the mind; with the tasks increased bit by bit, the mind is made stronger. Thus is Strength gained. By the tasks demanding exactness, the thoughts must not be scattered everywhere, but centered upon the thing to be done. Thus is Concentration gained. By making the hand work with care and a definite purpose, Skill is gained. By demanding of the thoughts that they must seek out all the qualities of an object, Attention is gained. By placing things and signs for things before us, we are taught to See. By educating us in sounds, we are taught to Listen. When we have a task that admits of a single correct result, we are taught Exactness.

Now, from all we have learned in these Talks about music it must be clear that all these qualities are just what are needed in music:

I. Strength of thought for Real doing.

II. Concentration for Right doing.

III. Skill for Well doing.

IV. Seeing and listening for the cultivation of Attention.

V. Correctness for the Manner of doing.

We sought for a simple lesson. It is this:

Let us learn all we can that is right and worthy for the strengthening of the mind, for the cultivation of the heart, for the good and joy of others; for these things are the spirit of music.

CHAPTER XXV.

THE CHILD AT PLAY

"When the long day is past, the steps turn homeward."

Once a child played on the sea-shore. The waves sang and the sand shone and the pebbles glistened. There was light everywhere; light from the blue sky, and from the moving water, and from the gleaming pebbles.

The little one, in its happiness, sang with the murmuring sea and played with the stones and the shells that lay about. Joy was everywhere and the child was filled with it.

But the day passed. And the little one grieved in its heart to leave the beautiful place. Delight was there and many rare things that one could play with and enjoy.

The child could not leave them all. Its heart ached to think of them lying there alone by the sea. And it thought:

"I will take the pebbles and the shells with me and I will try to remember the sunlight and the song of the sea."

So it began to fill its little hands. But it saw that after as many as possible were gathered together there were yet myriads left. And it had to leave them.

Tired and with a sore heart it trudged homeward, its hands filled to overflowing with the pebbles that shone in the sun on the sea-shore. Now, however, they seemed dull. And because of this, the child did not seem to regret it so much if now and then one fell. "There are still some left in my hands," it thought.

At length it came near to its home; so very tired, the little limbs could scarcely move. And one who loved the child came out smiling to welcome it. The little one went up close and rested its tired head; and opening its little hand, soiled with the sea and the sand, said:

"Look, mother, I still have one. May I go for the others some day?"

And the mother said:

"Yes, thou shalt go again."

And the child fell asleep to dream of the singing sea and of the sunlight, for these were in its heart.

APPENDIX

The following works are referred to in these Talks:

Addison, Joseph, "Spectator."

Alexander, Francesca, "Christfolk in the Apennine."

Antoninus, M. Aurelius, "Meditations."

Aristotle, "Ethics."

Bach, J.S., "The Well-tempered Clavicord."

Bach, J.S., "Kleine Präludien."

Baldwin, James, "Old Greek Stories."

Bacon, Francis, "Essays."

Bridge, J.F., "Simple Counterpoint."

Carlyle, Thomas, "Heroes and Hero-worship."

Cellini, Benvenuto, "Autobiography."

Epictetus, "Memoirs."

Grove, Sir George, "Dictionary of Music and Musicians."

Halleck, R.P., "Psychology and Psychic Culture."

Handel, G.F., "The Messiah."

Haupt, August, "Choralbuch."

Liszt, Franz, "Life of Chopin."

Lubbock, Sir John, "Pleasures of Life."

Luther, Martin, "Table Talk."

Mendelssohn, Felix, "Letters from Italy and Switzerland."

Parker, J.H., "ABC of Gothic Architecture."

Ruskin, John, "Queen of the Air."

Ruskin, John, "Sesame and Lilies."

Ruskin, John, "Val d'Arno."

Saintine, X.B., "Picciola."

Schubert, Franz, "Songs."

Schumann, Robert, "Album for the Voung."

Schumann, Robert, "Letters."

Schumann, Robert, "Rules for Young Musicians."

Tapper, Thomas, "Chats with Music Students."

Tyndall, John, "Glaciers of the Alps."

Tyndall, John, "On Sound."

Various Authors, "Les Maitres du Clavicin."

Xenophon, "Memorabilia."

Chats with Music Students

OR

TALKS ABOUT MUSIC AND MUSIC LIFE

BY

THOMAS TAPPER.

Price, Bound in Cloth, $1.50.

This volume appeals to every student of music, however elementary or advanced. It is designed to bring to the attention of those who make music a life-work, the very many contingent topics that should be considered in connection with music. To this end the subjects selected for the chats have a practical value, cover considerable ground, and are treated from the point of view that best aids the student. The reader is taken into confidence, and finds in the chapters of this work many hints and benefits that pertain to his own daily life as a musician.

NOTES:

1: From the "Table Talk."

2: Play to the children Schubert's song entitled "The Organ-man."

3: Phillips Brooks says in one of his sermons ("Identity and Variety"): "Every act has its perfect and entire way of being done."

4: Bohn edition, p. 35.

5: Read to the children such parts of Francesca Alexander's "Christ's folk in the Apennine" as seem to you pertinent.

6: John Ruskin, from the ninth lecture of "Val d'Arno."

7: John Ruskin. Third lecture of "Val d'Arno."

8: Franz Liszt's "Life of Chopin," Chapter V.

9: Ibid, Chapter VI.

10: "On Sound."

11: "On Sound" is referred to. The last paragraph of Section 10, Chapter II, may interest the children. The last two paragraphs of Section 13 are not only interesting, but they show how simply a scientist can write.

12: If the original is desired, see Tyndall's "Glaciers of the Alps."

13: Schumann wrote in a letter to Ferdinand Hiller, "We should learn to refine the inner ear."

14: From the sermon entitled "The Seriousness of Life."

15: Notice sometime how many of our English words have the Latin con.

16: See the fourth chapter of Reuben Post Halleck's "Psychology and Psychic Culture."

17: For instance, the subject of the C minor Fugue in the first book of "The Well-tempered Clavicord."

18: The subject of the C sharp minor Fugue.

19: The prelude in E flat minor and the subject of the G sharp minor Fugue.

20: Robert Schumann.

21: Quoted by Xenophon in the "Memorabilia," Book II, Chapter I, Bohn edition.

22: "Heroes and Hero Worship," Lecture I.

23: From the sermon entitled "Backgrounds and Foregrounds."

24: I should again suggest the value of letting the children become familiar with such books as J.H. Parker's "A B C of Gothic Architecture;" and of having always about plenty of photographs of great buildings, great men, great works of art and of famous places for them to see and to know ("letting them become familiar," remember).

25: See R.P. Halleck's "Psychology and Psychic Culture."

26: Read paragraphs 41 and 42 of John Ruskin's "Athena Chalinitis," the first lecture of "Queen of the Air."

27: John Ruskin, from the lecture entitled "Franchise," in "Val d'Arno," par. 206.

28: "Letters of Felix Mendelssohn Bartholdy from Italy and Switzerland." Letter of July 15, 1831.

29: "Letter of December 19, 1831."

30: Read also what is said of Chopin on p. 28.

31: Read to the children "The Wonderful Weaver" in "Old Greek Stories," by James Baldwin. It is only a few pages in length, and is well told.

32: Robert Schumann.

33: John Ruskin's "Queen of the Air," par. 102. ("Athena Ergane.") Read all of it to the children.

34: Idem.

35: Lord Bacon, from the essay "Of Great Places."

36: Robert Schumann.

37: Read John Ruskin's "Sesame and the Lilies," par. 19, and as much of what follows as you deem wise.

38: "The Ethics," Book IX, Chapter VII.

39: Always I have it in mind that the teacher will read or make reference to the original when the source is so obvious as in this case. The teacher's, or mother's, discretion should, however, decide what and how much of such original should be read, and what it is best to say of it.

40: I have not attempted to quote the exact words usually given.

41: Socrates. This quotation is from the "Memorabilia of Xenophon," Book I, Chapter VI.

42: Mary Russell Mitford.

43: "Autobiography of Benvenuto Cellini," Bohn edition, p. 23.

44: "The Miserere" of "Gregorio Allegri." It was written for nine voices in two choirs. "There was a time when it was so much treasured that to copy it was a crime visited with excommunication. Mozart took down the notes while the choir was singing it." (See Grove's "Dictionary of Music and Musicians." Vol. I, page 54.)

45: Dr. Bridge "On Simple Counterpoint." Preface.

46: Take, in August Haupt's "Choralbuch zum häuslichen Gebrauch," any simple choral. The one entitled "Zion klagt mit Angst und Schmerzen" is of singular beauty and simplicity.

47: Peters Edition, No. 200, page 11.

48: I should advise the teacher to have the two volumes entitled "Les Maitres du Clavicin." (They can be had in the Litolff collection.)

49: Op. 106.

50: "Der Erster Verlust" in Schumann's Op. 68 is well conceived in the sense that it is freely harmonic in some places, imitative in others, while in the opening the melody is very simply accompanied. Show the children how interesting the left-hand part is in this little composition.

51: From a Letter of the Spectator.

52: From the eighth paragraph of the Lecture entitled "Nicholas, the Pisan," in "Val D'Arno."

53: A blind beggar sitting on a bridge in an English town (it was Chester) many times astonished me with the rapidity of his hand-reading, and by the wonderful light of his face. It was wholly free from the perplexity which most of us show. It must arise in us from being attracted by so many things.

54: Eighty-first paragraph of "Val d'Arno."

55: Marcus Aurelius Antoninus, "The Meditations," Book V, Par. 34.

56: See footnote, p. 119.

57: From the thirteenth paragraph of the fourth book. I have changed the wording a very little to make it simple.

58: Sixteenth paragraph of the fifth book.

59: Essi quam videri.

60: "The Memorabilia."

61: "Epictetus," H.W. Rollison's Translation.

62: Plato.

63: Mozart wrote three symphonies between June 26th and August 10th, in the year 1778; and an Italian, Giovanni Animuccia, is said to have written three masses, four motettes, and fourteen hymns within five months. As an instance of early composition, Johann Friedrich Bernold had written a symphony before he was ten years of age, and was famous all over Europe.

64: Xenophon, "The Memorabilia," Book IV, Chapter VIII.

65: From the "Pleasures of Life." Eighth Chapter of the Second Series.

66: The little romance of N.B. Saintine is referred to.

67: Read to the children Chapter XIV in my "Chats with Music Students."

68: "Rules for Young Musicians."

Made in the USA
Middletown, DE
28 July 2019